CW01370463

Forfaiting for exporters

Forfaiting for exporters
practical solutions for global trade finance

Andy Ripley

INTERNATIONAL THOMSON BUSINESS PRESS
I(T)P An International Thomson Publishing Company

London • Bonn • Boston • Johannesburg • Madrid • Melbourne • Mexico City • New York • Paris
Singapore • Tokyo • Toronto • Albany, NY • Belmont, CA • Cincinnati, OH • Detroit, MI

Forfaiting for Exporters – Practical Solutions for Global Trade Finance

Copyright © Andy Ripley 1996

First published by International Thomson Business Press
I(T)P   A division of International Thomson Publishing Inc.
The ITP logo is a trademark under licence

All rights reserved. No part of this work which is copyright may be reproduced or used in any form or by any means – graphic, electronic, or mechanical, including photocopying, recording, taping or information storage and retrieval systems – without the written permission of the Publisher, except in accordance with the provisions of the Copyright Designs and Patents Act 1988.

Whilst the Publisher has taken all reasonable care in the preparation of this book the Publisher makes no representation, express or implied, with regard to the accuracy of the information contained in this book and cannot accept any legal responsibility or liability for any errors or omissions from the book or the consequences thereof.

Products and services that are referred to in this book may be either trademarks and/or registered trademarks of their respective owners. The Publisher and Author make no claim to these trademarks.

British Library Cataloguing-in-Publication Data
A catalogue record for this book is available from the British Library

First edition 1996

Produced by Gray Publishing, Tunbridge Wells, Kent
Printed in Great Britain by TJ Press (Padstow) Ltd, Padstow, Cornwall

ISBN   1-86152-036-0

International Thomson Business Press
Berkshire House
168–173 High Holborn
London WC1V 7AA
UK

International Thomson Business Press
20 Park Plaza
14th Floor
Boston, MA 02116
USA

http://www.thomson.com./itbp.html

Contents

Preface vii

PART ONE

Chapter 1 Background and history 1
Chapter 2 Discounting cash flows to net present value ... 15
Chapter 3 The mechanics of a forfaiting transaction 21
Chapter 4 Methods of discounting 35
Chapter 5 The discount rate and interest rate risk 41
Chapter 6 Credit risk 55
Chapter 7 Documentation and documentation risk 61
Chapter 8 How big is the forfaiting market? 87
Chapter 9 Accounting issues, profit and portfolio valuation ... 93

PART TWO

Chapter 10 Exporter's "how to" guide 109

PART THREE

Chapter 11 A case study 119
Chapter 12 What next? 131
Glossary 145
Appendix Approaches to calculating interest and discount rates ... 151
Index 163

Preface

Having been a practitioner in forfaiting in the late 1970s, and then returning to it in the mid-1990s, I find that there is an increasing appetite for a forfaiting finance textbook.

Particularly, there is currently a need for a "how to" manual from the exporter's perspective, for those exporters with customers in certain parts of south-east Asia, Latin America and eastern Europe. A number of excellent pamphlets have been published by financial institutions involved in the industry, however, this book seeks to go a step further by providing an A to Z for exporters who are considering using forfaiting as a means of assisting their customers by offering them credit terms. By using forfaiters the exporters can make the sale, receive cash up front, and do so without any recourse to themselves if the payment is not made by the obligor or guarantor at the payment date.

A characteristic of forfaiting is its flexibility in response to a wide range of financial needs. In view of this adaptability to a variety of situations it is not possible to provide a template for all occasions, so it is more appropriate to include a case study for illustrative purposes.

With the above in mind I have split the book into three parts.

- ❑ The first part looks at the background and history of non-recourse finance (forfaiting) (*Chapter 1*), discounting cash flows (*Chapter 2*), the mechanics of a forfaiting transaction (*Chapter 3*), methods of discounting (*Chapter 4*), the interest rate risk (*Chapter 5*), the credit risk (*Chapter 6*), the documentation risk (*Chapter 7*), the size of the market (*Chapter 8*), and accounting issues, profit and portfolio valuation (*Chapter 9*).
- ❑ The second part is a "how to" guide for exporters and outlines the likely process, methods and mechanics of how an exporter could use non-recourse finance (*Chapter 10*).
- ❑ Part three is a case study (*Chapter 11*).

Finally, *Chapter 12* considers the future for non-recourse financing.

I would like to thank Dr Andrew Bagley, William Hedley and Dylan Thomas for their guidance and all my colleagues at London Forfaiting Company PLC, particularly Doris Bloniarz, for their invaluable help and assistance. Any mistakes or omissions are mine.

I hope this book may be of use to anyone who has an interest in non-recourse trade finance and I will be particularly happy if it is of some practical use to exporters.

Andy Ripley
London
November 1996

ONE
Background and history

- 1.1 Introduction
- 1.2 Background
- 1.3 Selling and getting paid
- 1.4 À forfait finance
- 1.5 The birth of the à forfait finance market
- 1.6 The players
- 1.7 Market growth
- 1.8 Recent developments

1.1 Introduction

Forfaiting is the purchase of a trade debt or receivable, at a discount, without recourse to the exporter or previous holder(s) if the negotiable instrument evidencing the debt is not paid at maturity by the obligor or guarantor.

Forfaiting is a method of providing non-recourse short- and medium-term finance, usually at a fixed interest rate, to facilitate trade around the world.

However, if the non-recourse (or *à forfait*) trade transaction is defined by its historical characteristics, then a *possible* definition could be as follows:

> Non-recourse trade finance is a free-market, medium-term trade credit, for capital goods, arranged by a western manufacturer to an importer in an industrializing country which has limited access to hard currency. The trade credit is without recourse, fixed rate, usually bank guaranteed and is often evidenced by a series of negotiable bills of exchange or promissory notes repayable semi-annually.

Due to the flexible nature of the non-recourse credit instrument, any definition based on its characteristics is justifiably questionable.

However, it is a starting point and we will review these debatable definition characteristics throughout the book and then reconsider them in detail in Chapter 12. The present chapter outlines both the background and history of forfaiting and introduces the terms used in this starting-point definition.

Non-recourse trade credits first came to prominence in the 1950s. West European manufacturers of capital goods (such as machinery or machine parts) exporting to east European countries, were also required to provide the hard currency credits to the east European countries so that buyers could purchase the west European goods. Since the 1970s non-recourse trade credits have also been used as a method of funding western capital goods exports not only to east Europe but also to Latin America, south-east Asia, the Middle East and parts of Africa.

More recently forfaiting has been used to finance commodity and spare parts contracts on short terms (up to one year), in addition to capital goods. A further diversification has been to use non-recourse credit to provide working capital or longer term funding to companies without the associated purchase of goods. Flexibility in its application has been the key to the increasing use of forfaiting finance and it has continued to be adopted and adapted by the market as client requirements have changed over time.

1.2 Background

There is little new in the fundamentals of this type of finance, since forfaiting is merely the addition of the characteristic of non-recourse being appended to any negotiable credit instrument. For example, some variant of this type of financing may well have been used over 2000 years ago by Phoenician silk traders who, in order to make a sale, had to give their Athenian buyers credit, but at the same time traders wanted immediate cash payment.

The Phoenician trader (see Figure 1.1) made the sale to the Athenian buyer (1), accepted an IOU from the Athenian buyer for his silk (2), and then exchanged this IOU with a Levantine financier for a sum of cash (3), such that it was worthwhile for the Levantine financier to carry the risk on this transaction.

A plethora of trade finance credits as represented by the IOU with a range of legal jurisdictions and rights have been, and are currently being, used. However, there is a crucial element in these instruments. If at maturity (the payment date of the IOU) when the Levantine

Background and history 3

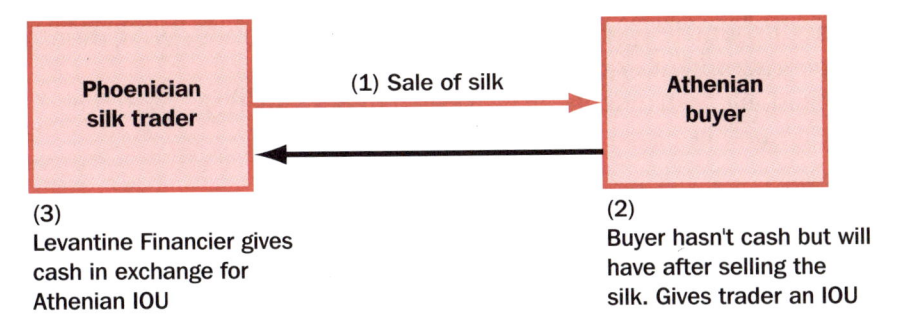

Figure 1.1 The underlying trade credit transaction.

[Diagram: Phoenician silk trader → (1) Sale of silk → Athenian buyer; (3) Levantine Financier gives cash in exchange for Athenian IOU; (2) Buyer hasn't cash but will have after selling the silk. Gives trader an IOU]

financier presents the IOU for payment to the Athenian buyer and it is not paid, then the Levantine financier has a right of recourse to the Phoenician trader for payment. However, if the IOU had been claused, "without recourse" then all parties including the Levantine financier would have agreed to give up any right of recourse against the Phoenician trader or any previous holders if the IOU was not paid on the due date. The right of recourse has been forfeited. Hence, *à forfait* in French, *forfaitierung* in German and *non-(or without) recourse* in English. These are all terms of reference for the increasingly used *forfaiting*, although historically the more familiar term, à forfait has been used.

There is no such thing as an *à forfait, forfaitierung, non-recourse* or *forfaiting* credit instrument. Forfaiting transactions use standard trade credit instruments (bills of exchange, promissory notes, deferred payment letters of credit). The only distinguishing factor with forfaiting is that the right of recourse, if the credit instrument is not paid on maturity, has been surrendered.

1.3 Selling and getting paid

As all sales staff know, be they traders, manufacturers, exporters, or even Phoenicians, making the sale may be the hard part of the equation but arguably as difficult is getting paid. Sales staff, having made a successful sale then hope to be in a position to repeat the sale at a later date. Suppliers are understandably very enthusiastic about cash payment before delivery and are reasonably content about cash on delivery, but they usually accept the fact that many transactions of value may well involve a period of credit. If the buyer/importer takes credit and pays later, either out of their own assets, or by increasing their other liabilities then there are a whole range of financial instruments that can be used to evidence the underlying debt. Statute in different countries varies, as does the nature and various obligations on the instrument evidencing the debt.

Negotiable instruments relating to an underlying trade transaction carry a number of risks:

1 credit risk
2 interest rate risk
3 documentary risk

Another example may help.

On 1 August 1694 a Sussex apple farmer is looking to sell his apples to a Covent Garden grocer (C. G. Grocer), who has no funds to pay the farmer until he has sold the apples. C. G. Grocer writes the farmer a note promising that in 90 days C. G. Grocer will pay the holder of the note £100 and then exchanges the note with the Sussex apple farmer for the apples. In 1694 this note would probably be referred to as an inland trade bill. During the following 300 years, variations of this note have been, and continue to be, used. The variations can be distinguished by their different names: bills of exchange, promissory notes, deferred payment letters of credit, book receivables and IOU's. Each will have their own characteristics and will be subject to a variety of rules and statutes in different countries. Most of this legislation is written to protect the holders, both existing and potential, of these credit instruments.

What are the risks facing the apple farmer?

❏ **The credit risk.** C. G. Grocer may not pay the note on the due date. **The farmer doesn't get paid.**

The credit risk, to use the jargon of twentieth-century American bankers, can be mitigated by getting a third party of perceived superior credit standing to C. G. Grocer to agree to pay the note if he doesn't pay on the due date. The third party will charge C. G. Grocer

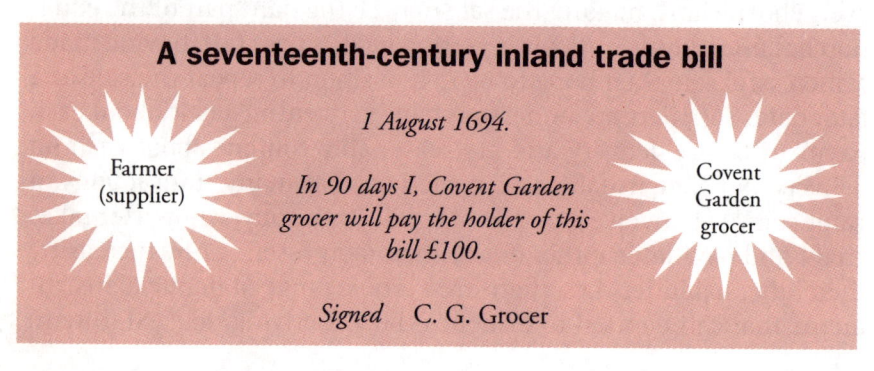

A seventeenth-century inland trade bill

1 August 1694.

Farmer (supplier)

In 90 days I, Covent Garden grocer will pay the holder of this bill £100.

Covent Garden grocer

Signed   C. G. Grocer

a fee for this guarantee. To the holder of the note (the farmer) there is still a credit risk, but it is now with the third party who has guaranteed the note. The credit risk of C. G. Grocer now lies with the guarantor.

❏ **The interest rate risk.** The farmer wants the cash for his apples now and doesn't want to wait 90 days for C. G. Grocer to meet the bill. So the farmer takes the guaranteed note to the 1694 version of a discount house. A discount house's primary function is to discount future cash flows to their present value (this is explored in more detail in Chapter 2). The discounting house gives the farmer a lower amount than the face value of the note in exchange for the note – say £95 cash (the price will depend on the discount rate used). The discount house then holds the note to maturity, when it will present the note to the farmer for payment.

If the discount house hasn't matched the 90 days (the tenor) with their funding of the asset they have acquired and interest rates then rise, they will be on the wrong side of an interest rate movement.

The revenue generated by the discount house holding the asset for the 90-day period, will be fixed at £5:

Face value of note at maturity – day 90	=	Cash given to farmer – day 1	=	Revenue to the discount house
£100	=	£95	=	£5

If the discount house borrowed the £95 for only 30 days to pay to the farmer on day 1, then the discount house will be running an interest rate risk. The discount house would have to borrow the £95 again on day 31 and if the cost of borrowing has increased, while the revenue remains fixed the discount house will see their profit margin eroded or even eliminated.

We can also identify an exchange rate risk if the asset is not matched in the same currency as the funding. Both of these risks are considered in some detail in Chapter 5.

❏ **The documentation risk.** In 1694 this note would need to comply with any existing statutory legislation. Care would also need to be taken regarding the good and honest *bona fides* of all parties to the transaction and that they are acting within the limits of their authority.

1.4 À forfait finance

À forfait finance can be associated with the types of trade credit finance similar to those used by the Phoenician trader over 2000 years ago and the Covent Garden grocer 300 years ago, such that there is an underlying obligation by the buyer and a receivable in the sellers' books of account, which is evidenced by a transferable note. The transaction can, subject to national statute, be evidenced by any of the instruments listed in Section 1.3. Forfaiting transactions have only one characteristic that fundamentally differentiates them from other forms of finance involving negotiable instruments evidencing an underlying receivable, which is:

> If the holder of the note, at maturity, presents the note to the buyer or the third party that guaranteed the note and the buyer and the guarantor fail to pay the note, the holder at maturity cannot present the note to any previous holders or the seller of the goods, for when the holder bought the note they forfeited the right of recourse to previous holders or the seller.

1.5 The birth of the à forfait finance market

In the early 1960s, east European Communist economies had little hard currency, but they did have an appetite for western, particularly West German, technology. Traditional trade credits had a tenor of up to six months. This may have been sufficient for commodity imports, but it did not allow a sufficient time for the east European importers to meet the hard currency payments on capital goods.

West German manufacturers of capital goods were looking to expand their markets, which included the Communist bloc. As their business with east European buyers was profitable, West German manufacturers were willing to wait up to five years for payment against negotiable trade credit instruments, which had been guaranteed by an east European state bank. However, the West German manufacturers did not have endless equity or access to sufficient debt funding to enable them to continue to offer these extended credits to their buyer in the developing eastern European market. The growth in the value of their receivables limited their ability to look for repeat business. What was to become a classic forfaiting transaction was formulated by West German manufacturers. This consisted of ten promissory notes with a tenor of five years repayable semi-annually in Deutschmarks (DM). This periodic repayment appealed to the east European importers, as it meant that they could obtain credit and repay their supplier out of cash flow over a period of time, rather than by a one-off bullet repayment.

Although these trade transactions were extremely profitable for the West German manufacturers, initially they generated no cash income as the revenue was in the form of a stream of receivables rather than cash. Unless the West German manufacturers could turn these receivables into cash, they were eventually constrained by a lack of liquidity which restricted the amount of this profitable trade they could undertake.

Central European financiers then took a key role in the evolution of the forfaiting market by agreeing to buy these trade paper assets from the West German manufacturers for cash. This generated cash for the manufacturers, allowing them to continue to develop this business and expand trade throughout the Comecon trading bloc.

Why did these Swiss, German and Italian financiers (forfaiters) agree to buy these assets? It certainly wasn't altruism. Quite simply, the forfaiters were willing to take a certain amount of the business at their risk, provided there was sufficient profit incentive and when they reached their own limits on the risk, they knew who would buy assets from them at a higher price than they had paid to the West German manufacturer. Like all traders, the forfaiters wished to follow the only rule for being a successful trader: *"buy low, sell high"*. However, there was one problem. Most of these original forfaiters were based in countries that had signed the International Convention for Commercial Bills (Geneva Convention 1930) – the effect of this is considered in more detail in Chapter 7. Briefly, however, the Geneva Convention ruled that holders of commercial bills at maturity had a right of recourse against all previous holders of the bill and ultimately the manufacturer, if the bill was not met on the due date.

The forfaiters liked the idea of buying low and selling high but did not like the idea of carrying a potential liability, in that the party to whom they had sold the receivable could claim payment from them in the event of the bill not being paid by the obligor or guarantor at maturity. This contingent liability would be on each bill they had handled until it was met at maturity. This reduced the appeal of the trade to the forfaiters. Consequently, in order to keep the trade simple, with no contingent liability to the original seller or any subsequent holder, each trade was set up in a way by which each seller and buyer of the debt agreed that they would surrender this right of recourse in the event that they were holding the bill at maturity and it was not paid by the importer or guarantor. So the exporter received cash for their receivables and in addition the exporter did not have any contingent liability. Thus, the forfaiting market was created. This is a good time to make the point that although there is no recourse on the bill/promissory note (except in cases of fraud), the exporter would be liable to the buyer under the terms of the main contract if, for example, the goods were defective. But the forfaiting contract is abstracted absolutely from the terms of the main sales contract between the exporter and importer.

The discount rate used to calculate the amount paid to the exporter (the present value of the note – see Chapter 2) reflected the forfaiters' perception of the credit risk, the interest rate risk, the documentation risk and the knowledge that there was no recourse to the exporter if the bill was not paid by the importer or guarantor on the due date. A new, but in reality ancient, trade instrument was not so much born as adapted and developed to reflect and respond to new requirements and the historic need for suppliers, traders, manufacturers, exporters and sales personnel to sell and get paid.

1.6 The players

So the forfaiting finance market in central Europe, developed because of an underlying need to find a way to allow trade to take place in the prevailing market circumstances. As in the case of many free markets and in order to satisfy these market needs, central European countries found it useful to accept an existing instrument specifically tailored for the purpose.

The key market circumstances were:

Western Europe	Eastern Europe
Free market economy	Command economy
Transferable currency. Liquidity enhanced by development of Euro currency markets	Non-transferable currency. Little liquidity or foreign exchange
Advanced technology	Basic technology
Exporters looking To new markets	An appetite for western goods

Exporters in Italy, Germany, the UK and Scandinavia were prepared to offer longer periods of credit than was usual, in order to make the sale, particularly as they would be paid in a western currency and the negotiable instruments evidencing the underlying debt were guaranteed by East German, Hungarian, Polish and other state finance institutions.

Eastern bloc command economies had control of all the limited foreign currency in their country and state bodies and institutions would direct those funds by reference to their individual central plan. However (as outlined in Section 1.5), in the exporters' balance sheet these assets were in the form of receivables, rather than cash, so limiting the exporters' access to cash and ultimately their ability to trade. Exporters therefore needed some mechanism to turn the long-term credit receivables into cash so they could continue to pay their suppliers and employees. The exports to eastern Europe were paradoxically becoming ever more profitable but the exporters were also becoming dangerously illiquid.

This can be summarized as follows:

Exporter	Importer
Wants to make sales	Appetite for machinery to manufacture goods to sell for foreign exchange (FX)
Prepared to give long credit terms	
Wants to make additional sales	All imports and FX tightly controlled by state
Needs assets in the form of cash and not term receivables	

There was an appetite among forfaiters, driven by profit margins, to purchase these term receivable instruments and consequently to generate cash for the exporters. However, because of the uncertainties of the underlying credit risk of the eastern bloc state banks, this trade would have merely transferred the illiquid receivable asset from the exporter to the forfaiter but for two factors.

First, the forfaiters once they had filled their own limits for a particular risk, knew where they could sell the receivable asset at a higher price than the price they would have to pay to the exporter for that receivable asset. Second, the notes evidencing the long-term receivables were traded without recourse. If the note was not met at maturity each previous holder of the trade instrument and the exporter would not be liable to meet the bill if the importer or guarantor failed to meet the trade instrument.

Exporter	Forfaiter
Needs assets in the form of cash and not term receivables	Willing to discount term receivables.
	Knew where and to whom they could on sell the receivable.
	Once the receivable is sold. There is no contingent liability.
	The words "without recourse" are added to the receivable instrument

In spite of the combination of a contingent liability associated with the recourse element of trade instruments and the lack of any track record of the eastern bloc guarantors, manufacturers, driven by thoughts of anticipated gross profit margins would often be prepared to run these risks. However, banks and debt lenders operating on much finer margins initially had little appetite for this east European state bank guaranteed trade credit paper until, crucially, the forfaiters began to find a secondary market for these instruments. In this secondary market the holders of the negotiable instruments could sell these instruments to other institutions.

The purchase and sale of the instruments was based on all parties being willing to give up any right of recourse against the exporter and previous holders, if the buyer or eastern bloc bank failed to meet the obligation at maturity. The exporter and all former holders had no contingent liability. The forfaiting finance market had emerged. This market could have sunk without trace but for the fact that eastern bloc banks built a reputation for meeting obligations on time and in full. This generated and developed both the primary and secondary market in forfaiting finance.

At this point it is appropriate to mention that there may still be a right of recourse/contingent liability if fraud occurs or if the documentation is not enforceable, such that free title cannot be assigned. This point is covered in more detail in Chapter 7.

1.7 Market growth

During the 1970 and 1980s, both the primary and secondary markets in and for non-recourse trade paper grew from its base of a small number of Italian, German, Swiss and London-based forfaiting institutions. Companies such as, Finanz AG, Trade Development Bank, Soditic, Monaval, Hungarian International Bank, Noreco, Fineurop and the leading West German deposit-taking banks shaped this non-recourse market and gave it a flexibility which, combined with the improving market perception of eastern European credit risk and thawing east–west political relations, enhanced its growth. Specialist banks, in addition to traditional deposit and clearing banks, developed forfaiting departments, usually within their trade finance sections. Sometimes these were successful and sometimes not – it depended on how the institution addressed, accessed and controlled three risks: credit, interest rate and documentation risk.

Later, specialist forfait houses were set up resulting in further growth and a perceptible geographic shift of the market from Switzerland and northern Italy to West Germany and more markedly to London. In 1984 London Forfaiting Company PLC, the only publicly owned and UK stockmarket-quoted specialist forfaiting company, was set up by Jack Wilson and Stathis Papoutes who had previously helped form and manage the Hungarian International Bank in London.

The primary forfaiting market (where the exporter and the original forfaiter organized the initial forfait transaction) was at first mainly used by exporters in developed countries to handle exports to countries perceived as being difficult risks to finance, for whatever reason, rather than as is sometimes thought, solely because of perceived payment problems. The primary forfaiting market has developed alongside state-backed export credit schemes, often as a competitor but also sometimes as an adjunct to the state export credit schemes. However, one significant reason for the growth in the popularity of forfaiting has been the gradual elimination of subsidies by state-backed export credit schemes under the Organization for Economic and Commercial Development's (OECD) consensus on government support for export credits.

Between market professionals a secondary market in non-recourse finance paper also evolved, which in effect *securitizes* these export receivables.

During the 1980s and 1990s an increasing awareness of the à forfait market has seen it develop a critical mass and momentum which has become self-generating. This growth, if it is to continue and develop, needs to be based on forfaiting being perceived as a cost effective and often more flexible user-friendly alternative for financing a transaction from the perspective of all the participants.

Market traders who evangelize the benefits of forfaiting will not see significant further development in the market, unless:

❏ exporters feel forfaiting is an effective alternative to finance their sales
❏ the importers believe it is an acceptable method of financing their purchases
❏ the discounters and holders feel the return warrants the risks
❏ guaranteeing banks can commercially justify their risk on the importer; and
❏ externalities do not restrict or limit international trade flows.

1.8 Recent developments

A recent development, particularly since the political changes in eastern Europe, has been the changed and changing perception and consequent stratification of geographic credit risk. Exporters in the Czech Republic are now using forfaiting to finance exports to other countries. Forfaiting is now as likely to be used to fund Czech machinery exports to Chile as, for example, German machinery exports to Poland. The underlying fact remains: suppliers, traders, manufacturers, exporters and salesmen, be they, Sussex apple farmers in 1694, Dusseldorf capital goods manufacturers in 1964 or Czech glass manufacturers in 1996, all want to sell and get paid, without any potential long-term legal or financial obligations.

The flexible nature of forfaiting has also led to its adoption for funding short-term (90–365 days) trade contracts. Commodities such as fuel and grain are sold on credit and the debt evidenced by promissory notes, bills of exchange or deferred payment letters of credit, which are discounted without recourse. Why? Because forfaiting suits the exporter, the importer and is appropriate to that particular transaction.

Another recent adaptation of non-recourse financing is its use to evidence a purely financial obligation, without any underlying trade deal (Chapter 12).

In the rest of the book we will examine discounting methods and the actual discount of a deal, the mechanics of the market, the market size, the primary and secondary markets, the three major risks, documentation, the practicalities of using this market and a view on its future. The book will focus particularly on the perspective of an exporter, but will also consider the position of the importer, guarantor and traders/holders of these non-recourse instruments, which relate to trade transactions and more recently, financial transactions.

Summary

❏ East–west European trade during the 1960s needed a mechanism to transfer hard currency from the importing eastern bloc economies to western capital goods manufacturers.

❏ Existing trade credit instruments were difficult to discount and carried a contingent liability to the exporter and successive holders, until the maturity date of the trade credit instrument.

❏ Exporters, driven by the potential of substantial gross profit margins, traded in eastern Europe until they ran into balance sheet liquidity problems.

❏ Central European financiers, who knew where to place the trade instruments but did not want any contingent liability, bought the receivables and sold them provided there was no recourse to the exporter or previous holders (which included themselves) if the instruments were not paid at maturity.

❏ The underlying debt in a forfaiting transaction can be evidenced by a variety of negotiable instruments but the essence of forfaiting is the surrender of the right of recourse by the holder at maturity, if the negotiable instrument is not paid on the due date by the importer or guarantor.

TWO
Discounting cash flows to net present value

2.1 Introduction
2.2 Price and (economic) value
2.3 The time value of money
2.4 Net present value
2.5 The internal rate of return
2.6 Financial instruments

2.1 Introduction

What is the current economic value of a non-recourse promissory note issued by the importer to the exporter? Why is the note's current economic value important?

The current economic value of the promissory note is important to the exporter, as this is the actual cash sum the exporter will receive for the sale of their goods or services if they discount the note in the primary forfaiting market. To the forfaiter, the current economic value of the note is the value at which the note could be traded in the secondary market or the sum at which it is valued (market value) in the forfaiter's books. This non-recourse promissory note is an asset to the holder whether they are the exporter, the primary forfaiter or any subsequent purchaser of the note. The note has an economic value and that value is its current market price.

2.2 Price and (economic) value

Oscar Wilde's often misquoted maxim about a cynic as

"a person who knows the price of everything and the value of nothing"

would be a tautology if the word "economic" was inserted in front of "value". In effect, "what is the current economic value of something?" is a rather laboured way of asking "what is its price?"

If we define a balance sheet asset as something that is expected to generate future economic benefit to an accounting entity at a point in time, then a non-recourse promissory note, held by the beneficiary, falls within this definition of an asset. The next step is to calculate the present value of the asset.

Fixed and current assets in a balance sheet represent values that are categorized and recorded in such a way that conforms with the accounting principles of prudence, objectivity, consistency and entity (see Chapter 9). In general fixed assets are held at historic cost less accumulated depreciation (subject to the intricacies in the UK of Financial Reporting Standard 5: other countries have their own accounting statutes and standards). Current assets are held at the lower of cost and market value which may be, but is not necessarily, the same as present (current market) value.

What is an asset currently worth in economic terms? We know it may coincidentally be the same as its balance sheet value. However, its present value is a function of either the price you can sell it for now (net realizable value), or the revenue stream the asset may generate for you now or at some time in the future (present value). Or by owning the asset, you can forgo a cost stream now or at some time in the future that you would have to pay if you didn't own the asset (replacement cost).

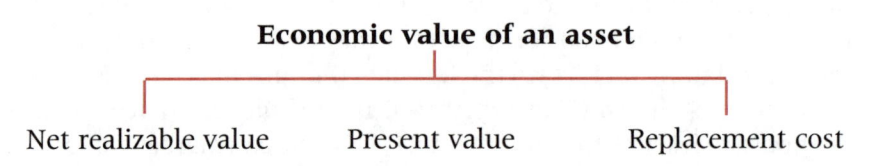

Economic value of an asset

Net realizable value   Present value   Replacement cost

The value of a non-recourse negotiable instrument to any particular holder is the present value of specific cash flows generated by the asset for its holder. The present value depends on the cash flows and the discount rate, which might vary from holder to holder. However, the present value of an asset is its economic value now or in the future, provided that the time value of money is taken into account.

2.3 The time value of money

By surrendering the use of your asset (cash) to another entity, that entity will pay you for the opportunity of being able to use your asset. The entity will also, hopefully, give you back the original asset (cash) and the price (normally cash) of borrowing that asset. The price is usually expressed as an annual percentage figure (interest rate) multiplied by the number of days you have surrendered the right to the asset over the number of days in a year, calculated on the amount of the asset (cash).

Usually, the longer you surrender the right to your money, the higher the interest rate. However, the price of borrowing cash (the interest rate) will be a function of supply and demand for funds at different periods of time.

Assume we invest 100 (A) now, with the interest rate curves over the time periods for fixed rates of interest illustrated in Figure 2.1.

At higher rates of interest, the longer the periods of surrendering your money (x axis), the principal (100) plus the compound interest (y axis) will increase. This is calculated by using the compound interest rate formula:

Principal = original amount
$$\times (1 + \text{annual rate of interest})^{\text{No. of years}}$$

$$P = A \times (1 + r)^t$$

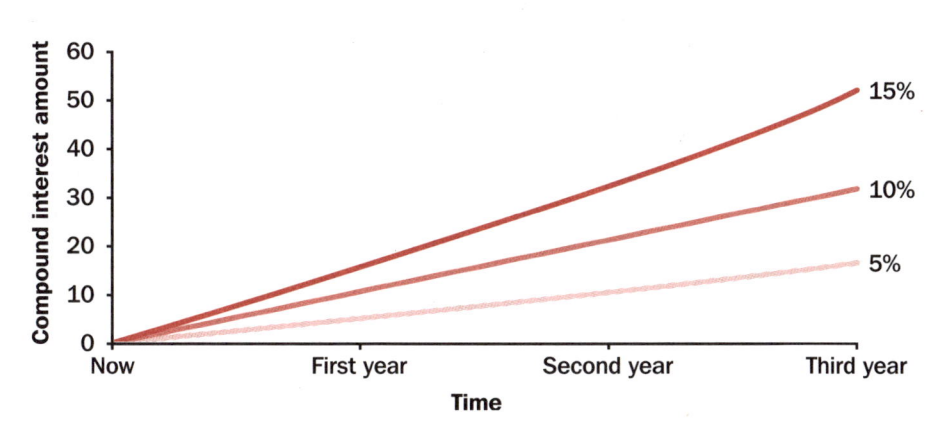

Figure 2.1 Interest rates.

18 Forfaiting for exporters

So the amount 100 (A) invested now, at a 15% per annum compound rate of interest will in three years time yield:

Principal		amount		interest
	=	100	×	(1.15) (1.15) (1.15)
	=	100	×	(1.5208)
	=	152.08		

The time value of money is based on the compound interest rate factor. In the example above this is 1.5208. We can calculate how much we expect to receive in the future (amount + compound interest) (P) if we multiply the amount invested today by the compounding factor.

The corollary of this is also true. If we know for certain we are to receive an amount P in the future, if we divide this amount (P) by the compounding factor, this will give us the present value of the principal net of the time value of money.

So, if we are to receive 152.08 in three years' time and we divide this by the compounding factor (15% per annum rate of interest now referred to as the discount rate) of 1.5208 then the present value of this future cash flow is 100.

2.4 Net present value

Discounting cash flows (DCF) to net present value (NPV) gives us a methodology that can be used to evaluate a range of investment decisions. The NPV in all cases is a function of two variables, the anticipated cash inflows/outflows and the discount factor.

These anticipated cash inflows and outflows and the discount factor can vary in their probability from being ill-informed guesses to almost cast iron certainties.

Let's take an example. Assume a car assembly line will cost 100 (asset cost and expenses, defined as $-I_0$) to buy and install now, at time 0. It is anticipated the net cash inflow generated by this investment over the next three years' will be t_1 (= 35), t_2 (= 45), t_3 (=55). We will also assume a given discount factor of 10% per annum.

$$\text{NPV} = -I_0 + (35/(1 + r)^{t_1} + 45/(1 + r)^{t_2} + 55/(1 + r)^{t_3})$$

$$= -100 + (35/1.10 + 45/1.21 + 55/1.33)$$

$$= -100 + (31.818 + 37.190 + 41.353)$$

$$\text{NPV} = +10.361$$

Using this example, as the resulting NPV is positive (+10.361) and this would increase the shareholder's wealth then this project should be undertaken.

Assuming the asset cost and expenses to be a constant at −100, by either reducing the per annum discount factor (10%) or increasing the future cash flows (35, 45, 55) the impact on the NPV will be to increase its size.

2.5 The internal rate of return

If you use a discount factor that brings the NPV of the cash flow exactly to zero then this discount rate is referred to as the internal rate of return (IRR). Using the figures from the previous example, by trial and error, we can calculate that, to two decimal places, the IRR is 15.35%.

To calculate the IRR

$$\text{NPV} = -I_0 + (35/(1 + r)^{t_1} + 45/(1 + r)^{t_2} + 55/(1 + r)^{t_3})$$
$$= -100.00 + (35/1.1535 + 45/1.3306 + 55/1.5348)$$
$$= -100.00 + (30.3424 + 33.8193 + 35.8353)$$
$$\text{NPV} = +0.0$$

Most spreadsheets/calculators will have a discounted cash flow (DCF) function. However, if you have to calculate the IRR by hand to sum the NPV to zero then as in this example you can round up the IRR to two decimal places or alternatively calculate the IRR to several decimal places.

2.6 Financial instruments

Capital investments, or project finance calculations, usually have a company discount rate to be used in investment calculations. This is set by the company and is a fixed figure, whereas the future revenue and cost streams need to be estimated by the project manager.

However, when we calculate the present value (PV) of financial instruments there is less scope for subjective value judgements. Each instrument will have attached to it the coupon to be paid (if any) on that instrument and the date and its redemption price (if any) and the date. These are fixed.

With non-recourse notes it is the face value at maturity which is fixed. However, the discount rate is estimated and will be based on the applicable interest rate yield curve and the credit standing of the entity that issued or guaranteed the notes. Based on this information we can calculate the investment we should make now (the current price) if we wish to buy those notes and their cash flow stream.

In Chapter 4 we will use the DCF to NPV technique to value forfaiting paper.

Forfaiting	Project finance
Discount rate is a derived figure	Discount rate is fixed
Revenue is fixed	Revenue is derived

Summary

- $P = A(1 + r)^t$ is the compound interest rate formula that takes into account the time value of money and interest given on interest across time periods.
- $A = P/(1 + r)^t$ is the discount rate formula that gives the compounded NPV of future inflows or outflows of cash.
- If the time period is fixed, the two variables are the discount rate used in the calculation (r) and the estimated future cash revenues or costs (P).
- With financial projects the discount rate is usually an internal company set rate and the estimated future cash inflows and outflows are estimated.
- With financial instruments and particularly non-coupon negotiable instruments such as forfaiting instruments the face or maturity value is fixed and the discount rate is the variable.

THREE

The mechanics of a forfaiting transaction

3.1 Introduction
3.2 The underlying trade contract
3.3 The forfaiting proposal
3.4 Terms and conditions
3.5 The primary and secondary markets

3.1 Introduction

This chapter details the mechanics of a basic forfaiting transaction. The terms and conditions used in the example are presented in Section 3.3, and Section 3.4 attempts to explain and define the terms and conditions. The characteristics of both the primary and secondary forfaiting markets are also considered.

3.2 The underlying trade contract

It is spring 1996, a British manufacturing company (Botplantco), which sells bottling machinery, is negotiating a contract to supply a bottling plant to a Czech soft drinks company (CZ) in Prague (Figure 3.1). The contract value is £1,000,000 and the buyer does not have sufficient funds to pay Botplantco on delivery of the plant.

As CZ, the Czech importer, currently hasn't the cash to pay for the machines and doesn't want to draw on loan facilities at their bank, they need credit on terms acceptable to them. CZ can afford to pay a 10% down-payment but requires credit over a two-year period for the balance of the plant, with four semi-annual instalments. CZ has offered to pay interest at a rate of 7% per annum on the reducing

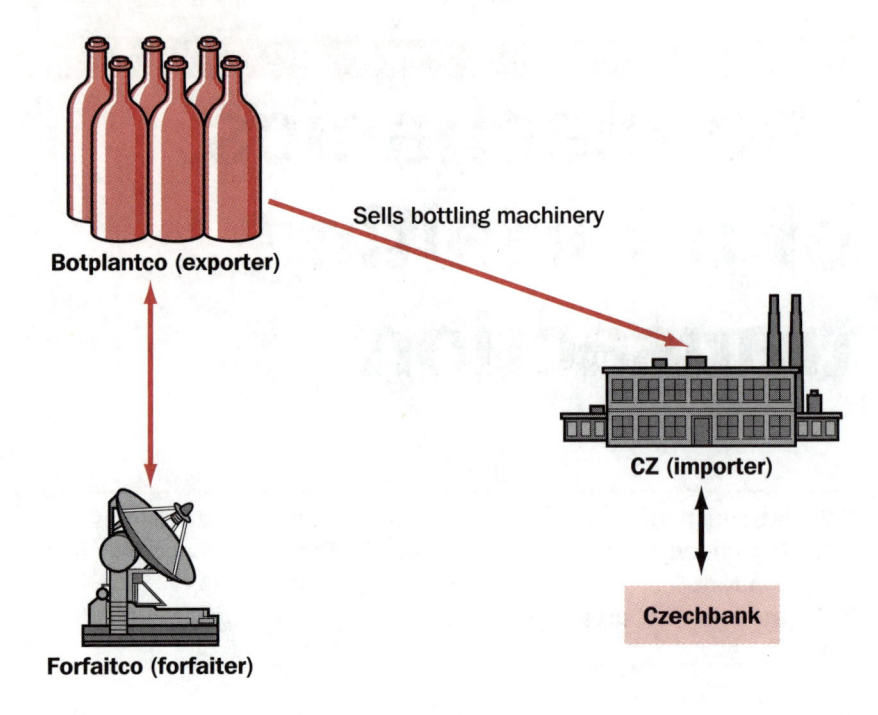

Figure 3.1 Illustration of a forfaiting transaction.

outstanding amounts. CZ has the support of their local bank (Czechbank) who will guarantee the payment of the instalments. Czechbank will charge CZ a guarantee fee, usually calculated over the credit period on the outstanding amounts. Botplantco have investment plans of their own and do not wish to tie up their own capital, funding CZ's business and therefore they speak to a forfaiting company (Forfaitco).

The date is now 1 March 1996 and Botplantco advises Forfaitco that they expect to finalize a contract with CZ on 1 April and would expect to deliver the plant four months later. From experience Forfaitco estimates that for this market it would usually take two weeks, following delivery, in order to obtain and finalize the documentation for discount. Forfaitco then provides Botplantco with an indicative proposal.

3.3 The forfaiting proposal

From: Forfaitco
Importer:
Guarantor:
Re:

To: Botplantco
CZ (Czech Republic soft drinks company)
Czechbank
sale of bottling plant

Basis of calculation

Currency	Sterling
Required amount	1,000,000
Down-payment	10%
Number of bills	4
Interest paid by importer (per annum)	7%
Method of interest calculation	twelfths
Commitment date	1/4/96
Interest/shipment date	31/7/96
Discount date	14/8/96
Commitment fee (per annum)	0.75%
Days of grace	3
Method of discounting	straight discount
Discount rate	6.875924%
Equivalent semi-annual yield	7.375%

Summary of calculation

	£
Contract value	1,000,000.00
Down payment	100,000.00
Principal – *term of reference in market*	900,000.00
Interest	78,750.00
Total face value	978,750.00
Discounted value	897,778.02
Total proceeds to exporter	997,778.02
Commitment fee (135 days)	2,715.03
Final proceeds	995,062.99

Bill details

No.	Maturity	Principal	Interest	Face value	Net value
1	31/1/97	225,000.00	31,500.00	256,500.00	248,140.67
2	31/7/97	225,000.00	23,625.00	248,625.00	232,044.93
3	31/1/98	225,000.00	15,750.00	240,750.00	216,259.47
4	31/7/98	225,000.00	7,875.00	232,875.00	201,332.95
		900,000.00	78,750.00	978,750.00	897,778.02

At this stage, an indicative proposal is probably sufficient for Botplantco, as they are not certain whether they will be able to finalize a contract on the terms detailed. However, if required, Forfaitco could offer a firm proposal at this point. This option arrangement is detailed in Section 3.4.2.

Continuing on the basis of the indicative proposal put forward by Forfaitco, as outlined, Forfaitco have indicated their willingness to finance the transaction on the terms quoted, purchasing the two-year debt from Botplantco. Based on market practice for each country, Forfaitco will outline the type of negotiable instruments which would be acceptable for the transaction and this will form the basis of one element of the negotiations between Botplantco and CZ.

Referring to the proposal, we see that the parties to the transaction are identified and the details of any necessary guarantor are shown. The basis of calculation sets out the basics of the potential forfaiting contract, being the currency, value, any down-payment, the credit period/number of repayments and any interest rate payable by the buyer. The estimated date for finalization of the contract with the buyer and the commitment by the forfaiting company are shown and the scheduled delivery and estimated discount dates are detailed. Finally, in this section of the proposal, the forfaiting company sets out their terms for discounting the transaction, the commitment fee, any days of grace and the method of discounting and the applicable discount rate quoted.

The summary of calculation shows the exporter the amount they can expect to receive from the forfaiting company, based on the estimated dates used in the calculation. The exact amount will vary if any of the dates change.

The bill details section of the proposal show the maturity dates of the repayments, based on the scheduled delivery date, the amount of principal and interest payable by the buyer and the amount the forfaiting company will pay for each of the bills (based on the estimated discount date shown in the calculation).

Using this proposal, Botplantco will continue negotiations with CZ. Any amendments or changes to the basis of the contract during negotiations can be referred to Forfaitco for them to revise their proposal.

Let us assume that everything proceeds as planned and the forfaiting contract is signed and made effective on 1 April 1996. Forfaitco's view of the market is unchanged and sterling interest rates over the two years' credit period have remained the same. Forfaitco now provides Botplantco with a firm offer to finance the contract, setting out a final date by which they must receive the agreed documentation for discount. In practice this final date should cover the scheduled delivery period, the estimated documentation time and a period to allow for potential delays in manufacture, delivery and processing of documentation. Botplantco sign the forfaiting contract and accept the firm offer from Forfaitco.

Botplantco is committed to sell the transaction to Forfaitco and Forfaitco is committed to purchase the transaction from Botplantco without recourse, within the time scale agreed, subject to their receipt of the agreed documentation.

Having detailed this basic forfaiting proposal, let us now go back and consider the terms and conditions given in this proposal. At this stage it is also probably worth reminding ourselves of two points.

First, the non-recourse aspect of forfaiting means that Forfaitco, or any subsequent holder of the negotiable instruments covering the four semi-annual instalments, will have no right of recourse against Botplantco or any previous holder of the instruments, if the importer CZ or Czechbank fail to pay any of the instruments on their maturity dates.

Second, as forfaiting is flexible there is no standard format or set terms and conditions. Both the forfaiter and the exporter can mutually agree on their own terms and conditions that are acceptable to them and are not against the laws or statutes that govern each party. However, the terms and conditions used in this example are commonly used in the majority of forfaiting transactions.

3.4 Terms and conditions

The terms used to express the supplier credit provided by Botplantco to CZ are for the most part self-explanatory. As would usually be the case, the interest rate paid by CZ has been charged from the date of shipment, up to each maturity date and has been calculated on the reducing outstanding amounts of the debt. The interest has been calculated on a simple annual rate basis, with each full month of credit attracting one-twelfth of the annual rate. (The alternative would have been to charge interest on a daily basis, where it is customary to use a 365-day year for sterling contracts and a 360-day year for other currency contracts.)

3.4.1 Commitment fee

The proposal (Section 3.2) is based on Botplantco finalizing a contract with CZ and agreeing a commitment with Forfaitco on 1 April 1996, delivery being made on 31 July 1996 (four months later) and discount taking place on 14 August 1996 (two weeks after delivery) (see Figure 3.2a).

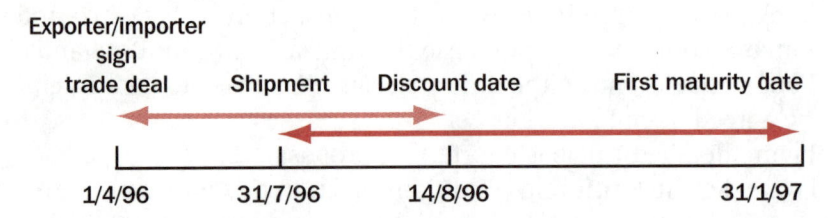

Figure 3.2(a) An illustrative forfaiting transaction – the relevant dates.

Forfaitco has committed to purchase the debt (90% of contract value plus interest, i.e. a total of £978,750) from Botplantco and Forfaitco will set this amount against its limits for the particular guarantor and or country limits it has set for business in the Czech Republic. For a particularly difficult market, having agreed a commitment for a contract may prevent the forfaiting company from taking further business in that market until the debt is repaid or the forfaiting company manages to sell the debt to another institution or investor. In many cases the forfaiting company also fixes the discount rate when a commitment is agreed, thereby running a risk of interest rates increasing over the commitment period. To cover the potential guarantor, country and interest rate risks, the forfaiting company will usually charge the exporter a commitment fee, calculated on the amount for which the commitment is agreed and payable from the date of commitment until the date discount takes place. In our example, Forfaitco has quoted a commitment fee of £2715.03 (0.75% per annum calculated on £978,500 from 1 April 1996 to 14 August 1996 – a period of 135 days). The timing of the payment of the commitment fee will be agreed between the forfaiting company and the exporter and will be dependent on the details of each individual transaction.

So, in summary, what is the commitment fee for?

1. Part of the future balance sheet of the forfaiter must be allocated to the transaction that the forfaiter has agreed to in issuing the commitment.

2 Giving a commitment at a certain price and subject to the terms and conditions of that agreement means that the issuer is now carrying both the interest rate risk and the credit risk.
3 On what are perceived as small deals there is a tendency (although less so in the UK) to charge flat fees by the forfaiter. The tenor of a commitment can be for any period both parties are agreeable to, however over six months would be considered long.
4 Counterparties are particularly important because if interest rates or credit margins move during the tenor of the commitment then parties to the agreement must be able to trust the counterparties to stand by their agreement. "My word is my bond" is still a crucial part of forfaiting and litigation is, thankfully, presently unusual, although everything is documented soon after verbal agreement.

3.4.2 Options

Where an exporter is confident of finalizing a contract in a more difficult market, for which the forfaiting company may have limited capacity, the exporter may require the forfaiting company to commit to finance the business prior to the contract being signed. This is usually referred to as an option. Typically, this could take the form of a firm commitment, incorporating a clause which gives the exporter the right to cancel the commitment on a fixed date in the event of certain circumstances, for example, failing to sign the contract, non-receipt of a down-payment or failure to make a contract effective. This arrangement gives the exporter the piece of mind that they can finalize a contract within the agreed time scale, in the knowledge that non-recourse finance is available and at the same time limits the cost of the commitment fee to the option period. In our example, Botplantco could have agreed an option on 1 March 1996, allowing them to cancel the commitment on 1 April 1996 in the event that they did not finalize a contract by that date. An option fee would be

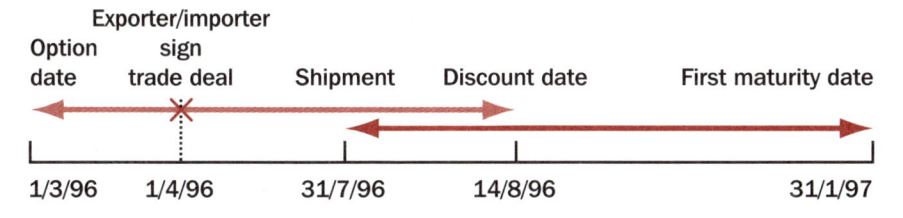

Figure 3.2(b) An illustrative forfaiting transaction – including the option.

negotiated between the forfaiting company and the exporter: using the commitment fee level of 0.75% per annum in our example, this would cost Botplantco £623.45 (0.75% per annum calculated on £978,750 from 1 March 1996 to 1 April 1996 – a period of 31 days).

3.4.3 Methods of discounting

Much of the mystique and a good deal of the misunderstanding of forfaiting can be attributed to the confusing number of various methods of discounting that can be used to calculate the proceeds paid to exporters or previous holders of a debt: semi-annual yields, straight discounts, annual yields, simple yields and discount to yields, to name the most usual. A more comprehensive analysis can be found in Chapter 4, but at this point a simple comparison of a discount to yield rate and a straight discount rate will suffice.

In simple terms, a discount to yield rate is the rate of return or yield the forfaiting company is looking for on the amount they are paying for the debt. (The purchase price or the proceeds they are paying to the previous holder.) "Semi-annual" denotes any compounding of the rate of return on a six-monthly basis over the period of the credit.

By comparison, the calculation of a discount on a straight discount rate basis is simple although it takes no account of the true value of money. A straight discount rate is applied to the face value of each payment and is calculated on a simple basis from the date of discount, until the maturity date of each repayment.

Any given straight discount rate would give the forfaiting company an equivalent discount to yield rate of return, compounded semi-annually or otherwise. Forfaiting companies may quote straight discount rates because they are easier to understand. The fact that straight discount rates are calculated on the higher face value of the debt, whereas discount to yield rates show the rate of return expressed as a percentage of the lower discounted proceeds figure, means that equivalent straight discount rates are always lower than their corresponding discount to yield rate. When exporters are obtaining competing quotations, it is important that they compare discount rates on the same basis.

3.4.4 The discount rate

Forfaitco has quoted a straight discount rate of 6.875924 per annum which will give them a rate of return or semi-annual yield of 7.375% per annum. In calculating their required rate of return, Forfaitco will consider two fundamental points. First, what the borrowing costs would be for the currency and credit period of the transaction together with the margin they require to cover their perception of the risks involved (i.e. the credit risk, the interest rate risk and the documentation risk). Second, what they believe the secondary market appetite will be for the transaction, taking into account the credit and interest rate risks which may apply during the commitment period (i.e. what do they think they will be able to sell the transaction for, once they become holders of the debt).

An analysis of Forfaitco's considerations might show the following.

First, the Sterling borrowing costs for the average life of the two-year credit period – using the London Interbank Offered Rate (LIBOR) – is 6.625% per annum, plus a margin of almost 0.75% to cover the risks detailed above. Second, the current secondary market price for the transaction might be 7.125% per annum semi-annual yield, giving a potential profit of 0.25% per annum on the deal, assuming interest rates and market sentiment remain unchanged over the commitment period.

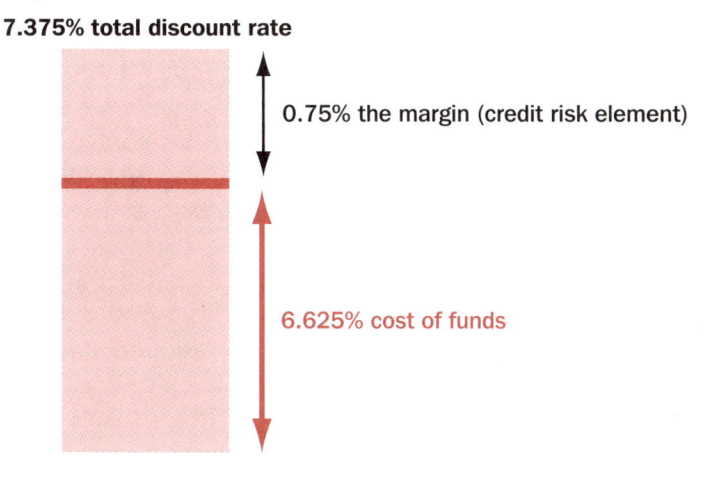

7.375% total discount rate

0.75% the margin (credit risk element)

6.625% cost of funds

As most people involved in the forfaiting market will admit, there is no exact science in pricing a forfaiting transaction. The successful participants may tell you that you need to have a "feel" for the market but history can tell a different tale. How many past participants misread the Russian market in the 1980s and the Iranian market in the early 1990s and paid the price?

First maturity date: 31/1/97

From 14/8/96 (discount date) to 31/1/97 (maturity date) plus three days of grace = 173 days

£256,500 (face value) × 6.875924% per annum × 173/365 = £8359.33

£256,500 − £8,359.33 (discount cost) = £248,140.67 (net value to exporter)

(Discounting is covered in some detail in Chapters 2, 4 and the Appendix.)

3.4.5 Days of grace

Days of grace are the number of days a forfaiting company adds to each maturity date in calculating discounted proceeds to be paid to the exporter or previous holder of the debt. They could be described as the period the forfaiter believes it will take in order for them to receive payment beyond the actual maturity date. In our proposal Forfaitco has quoted three days of grace. If payment is received on the actual maturity date, Forfaitco will "earn" three days interest as additional profit. If payment is not received until five days after the maturity date, Forfaitco has a potential two-day interest "loss", as they have waived all rights of recourse to Botplantco. In practice, Forfaitco, or the holder of the note at maturity, may demand delay interest from CZ and/or Czechbank, depending on the amount and period involved.

Some critics argue that forfaiting companies use days of grace as a mean of increasing their rate of return on a transaction and put forward the argument that the forfaiter should simply quote a discount rate for the transaction. The forfaiting company may respond by suggesting that the overall pricing is taken into account in determining the market's appetite for the risk.

3.4.6 Number of bills/notes

In our example there are four bills of exchange in the series. However, the classic forfaiting transaction for capital goods will normally consist of ten non-recourse promissory notes, a note becoming due every six months from the date of shipment. However, there are considerable variations on this format. It may suit the exporter if he or she has no need of cash to hold the notes for a year, receive the payment on the first two notes from the importer and then discount the remaining eight notes for cash with a forfaiter. The underlying trade transaction may be for only three years with six notes payable six-monthly or fewer notes over a longer time. The underlying trade may be for oil imports needing only six month's credit in which case there may well be only one note, or if it is a sizeable figure there may be ten notes or series of notes each with the same tenor and value but breaking the trade down into more manageable notes to discount in the secondary market.

The flexibility of forfaiting between its practitioners is one of the reasons, along with its non-recourse characteristic, for its increasing use.

3.5 The primary and secondary markets

The trade finance deal we have considered in this chapter falls comfortably into what would be referred to as the primary market. There are two trading parties to the trade, in this case the British bottling machinery exporter Botplantco and the Czech importer CZ.

Through the use of a non-recourse negotiable instrument, terms have been made available to CZ by the forfaiting house Forfaitco. Botplantco receives a discounted cash sum (£995,062.99) on transfer of clean documentation to Forfaitco, who owns the future obligation of CZ, which is evidenced by the four bills of exchange.

These bills of exchange are an asset that can be held by Forfaitco to maturity or can be sold on to a third party at a mutually agreed price. This buying and selling between successive holders in due course at varying discount rates is referred to as the secondary market.

It may seem rather trite to state the fact but both the primary and secondary markets, like any market, attract a variety of participants with widely differing objectives and structures. For example, in the secondary market large, deposit gathering banks with a network of well-established client relationships such as German house banks with a knowledge and familiarity of forfaiting may well make this type of non-recourse funding available to their clients and hold the notes to maturity. The German house bank may not wish their client's name or paper to be circulated in the market. Whereas a similar institution may feel it wishes to provide a service to a valued client but may not wish to hold the credit risk of the particular bank guaranteeing the importers liability and will make use of the secondary market.

In the 1970s some centralized state institutions (e.g. Banque Exterieur d'Algerie in Algeria) which guaranteed importers' future obligations would sometimes place restrictions on the transferability of notes in the secondary markets. This was done in the belief that this state-guaranteed trade receivable would not satisfy the appetites of potential lenders looking for syndicated country loans. For this reason some banks still make their guarantees non-transferable or make assignment difficult.

This book is aimed largely at exporters and the primary market is the main area of interest. However, there is an obvious, albeit changing and dynamic, relationship between both markets.

There are a number of factors that are currently impacting the secondary forfaiting market. Paradoxically the reasons responsible for the growth of this market are in part the same factors resulting in a reduction in the volumes in trading in the secondary market.

Although a growing primary market is generating more forfaiting paper, the maturity of the market, the growth in methods of mitigating risk, the range of exotic financial assets available to investors and the current fashion for emerging market assets has seen a contraction in the trading of forfaiting paper in that generators and holders of the paper at this point in time appear to be increasingly prepared to run with and offset the risks associated in holding this paper rather than trading it.

It appears to be the case that there is a developing primary market which is in part based on an increasing familiarization with forfaiting and in the secondary market there is more of this paper about, both in value and volume terms, but it is held rather than traded. None of this can be substantiated, however, as there is at present no publicly available statistical information to quantify either the primary or secondary forfaiting markets.

Factors enhancing the growth of the secondary market

- Since the 1980s financial assets have increasingly been bundled up and sold off to third parties. This process of the securitization of assets through a secondary market has meant that financial institutions are increasingly familiar with the division between the generator of assets and the ultimate holder of those assets to maturity.
- The growth of a range of hedging instruments through the derivatives markets has meant risks, both actual and perceived, in holding a particular asset can be mitigated by the use of those markets.
- Emerging markets, at the time of writing, are increasingly seen as areas of opportunity. (The now politically incorrect term "less-developed countries" and memories of syndicated sovereign loan bad debts would appear to have momentarily faded.)
- The growth of high-yield fixed rate paper debt instruments in the US in the 1980s, on liquid, but even by prudent accounting methods often insolvent companies, led to the creation of financial traders apparently prepared to make a bid on high-risk assets in all sorts of non-performing secondary loan markets.
- The conversion of debt into equity and the variety of financial instruments in the Eurocurrency markets make non-recourse trade finance instruments look rather staid by comparison.
- The volatility of capital markets in the first quarter of 1994 was far greater in the financial instrument Eurobond market (a price variation of between −2% to −20%) than in the trade instrument forfaiting market for the same perceived risk (a price variation of between −2.5% to −10%).

Summary
Primary market

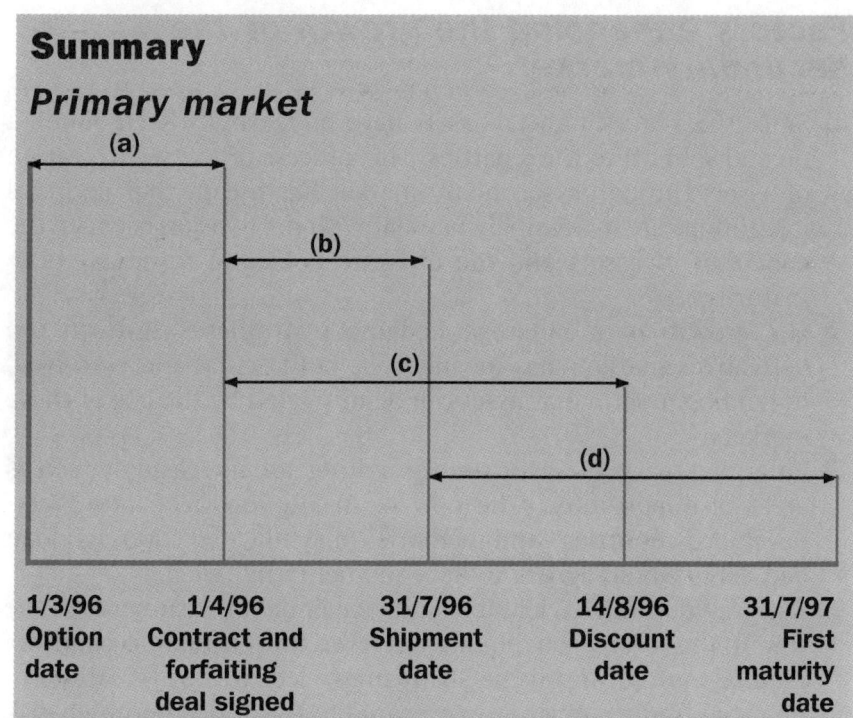

1/3/96	1/4/96	31/7/96	14/8/96	31/7/97
Option date	Contract and forfaiting deal signed	Shipment date	Discount date	First maturity date

(a) **Option period** – if required, the forfaiting company may give the exporter a firm offer of finance prior to the sales contract being signed (see Section 3.4.2).

(b) **Manufacturing/delivery period** – period from signature of contract to date of shipment.

(c) **Commitment period** – period from the date the forfaiting company and the exporter agree a commitment until the date the forfating company purchases the transaction (see Section 3.4.1).

(d) **Credit period** – period over which the exporter has extended credit to the buyer and the period for which interest (if any) is charged by the exporter to the buyer.

Secondary market

The secondary market has grown in line with the primary market, but forfaited paper would appear to be traded less. The maturity of the market, the range and methods of mitigating holding risks, the recent emergence of far riskier financial instruments and the relatively low margin volatility has led to an increasing willingness to hold non-recourse trade-based paper. Added to which the primary forfaiters are more likely to place paper with end investors than previously.

FOUR
Methods of discounting

4.1 Introduction
4.2 Methods of discounting
4.3 The trader's perspective
4.4 The exporter's perspective

4.1 Introduction

In the secondary forfaiting market, whatever negotiable instrument is used, the face value at maturity is a fixed amount. So its current price is a function of the discount rate used and the method of discounting. The discount rate used will need to reflect all the risks associated with that unique negotiable instrument. These risks are relatively easy to classify and are covered in Chapters 5–7. Of course, the hard part is quantifying the risk and translating the risk, through the discount rate to be used.

Having considered the mechanics of discounting future cash flows to their net present value (NPV) in Chapter 2, we will consider in this chapter the various methods of discounting and quantify their impact on the current market price of a forfaited note.

4.2 Methods of discounting

In Chapter 2 we discounted a promissory note to its present value (PV) using the discount formula

$$\text{PV amount} = \frac{\text{face value of note to be discounted}}{(1 + \text{discount rate})^{\text{time period}}}$$

So that a note worth £10,000 in three years' time at a discount rate of 12% per annum has a PV of £7117.94

$$= \frac{10{,}000}{(1+0.12)(1+0.12)(1+0.12)}$$

$$= \frac{10{,}000}{(1.4049)} = £7117.94$$

If the face value of a note is fixed then the PV of a note will vary according to both the discount rate and the method of discounting used. However, for the purpose of these examples let us assume both a constant discount rate of 12% per annum and a note with a face value of £10,000 in three years' time.

The example above uses a discount factor based on compounding the discount rate annually. Often the discount rate used will be discounted to yield semi-annually. Using the same given figures, if the only variable is to use a semi-annual rather than an annually compounded discount rate, the PV can be calculated as follows:

$$= \frac{10{,}000}{(1+0.06)(1+0.06)(1+0.06)(1+0.06)(1+0.06)(1+0.06)}$$

$$= \frac{10{,}000}{(1.4185)} = £7049.70$$

When the discount rate is calculated semi-annually the PV is £7049.70 rather than £7117.94 if the discount is calculated annually. Similarly, if the compounding period is reduced further, either quarterly or monthly, then the PV is further reduced.

It is currently a convention in the market that the word "yield" refers to the discounting technique. So using the same example with varying discount periods but a fixed discount rate to yield, the respective PVs would be as follows:

❑ *Simple discount to yield at 12% per annum for three years face value £10,000*

In this instance, using the given time period (three years), discount rate (12% per annum) and maturity value (£10,000). The simple discount to yield would be the maturity value divided by the aggregate of the per annum discount rates without compounding this discount rate.

Methods of discounting

- *Simple discount to yield at 12% per annum for three years face value £10,000.*

$$PV = 10,000/1.36 = £7352.94$$

- *Annual discount to yield at 12% per annum for three years face value £10,000.*

$$PV = 10,000/(1.12)^3 = 10,000/1.4049 = £7117.94$$

- *Semi-annual discount to yield at 12% per annum for three years face value £10,000.*

$$PV = 10,000/(1.06)^6 = 10,000/1.4185 = £7049.70$$

- *Quarterly discount to yield at 12% per annum for three years face value £10,000.*

$$PV = 10,000/(1.03)^{12} = 10,000/1.4257 = £7,014.09$$

Straight discount

There is also what is referred to as the straight discount rate, as used in the example in Chapter 3. This has nothing to do with discounting cash flows to their PVs but is a simple method of calculating the current price, which takes no account of the time value of money. Again using the same example

- *Straight discount at 12% per annum for three years face value £10,000. Current price = £6400.*

This method is to take the annual interest on the face value, calculate the sum over three years and subtract it from the face value. This is equivalent to an internal rate of return (IRR) yield of marginally over 16%.

> This has nothing to do with discounting cash flow (DCF) or the time value of money, using our example the simple method of taking 12% per annum off the maturity value of the negotiable instrument to give a current dealing price. This is £10,000 less £1200 + £1200 + £1200 = £6400.

4.3 The trader's perspective

The basis of any trade, as mentioned earlier, is to "buy low, sell high". Therefore a trader looking to buy a three-year negotiable instrument with a given maturity value of £10,000 and a discount rate of 12% per annum will want to calculate the purchase price using the straight discount method at £6400 and sell, using a simple discount to yield at £7352.94 (see Figure 4.1). The trader is concerned with the in and out price. By decreasing the tenor of the compounding period you will increase the discount rate and consequently decrease the PV of the negotiable instrument.

Compounding period	Simple	Annual	Semi-annual	Quarterly	Monthly
Face value	10,000	10,000	10,000	10,000	10,000
Discount factor	1.36	1.4049	1.4185	1.4257	1.4308
NPV	7352	7118	7050	7014	6989

Figure 4.1 PV discount-to-yield table for three years at 12% per annum on a note with a maturity value of £10,000.

The trader may also wish to hold the note to run it for yield, provided he or she can obtain funds over the note's lifetime at less than the interest rate of return obtained in holding the note.

4.4 The exporter's perspective

Although a generalization there is more than an element of truth in the statement that the exporter's sales staff want to make a sale to obtain their commission. That commission could be based on the face value or the PV of the sales contract, it depends on the particular sales incentive scheme operated by the exporter. Whereas sales commission schemes really only reach an art form when tied into wholesale and retail sales, even for capital goods the sales staff's commission is usually a powerful sales incentive. The sales staff are interested in closing the sale, hitting their sales targets and associated commission, and achieving the company's sales objectives. They are probably not directly concerned with gross profit margins or overheads.

However, the managers and directors of the exporting company have an objective to maximize the shareholder's wealth over time.

Methods of discounting 39

The company needs to make the sale, but for them it has to be at a price that gives them an acceptable gross profit margin and as a minimum, covers the overheads of the business to generate a net profit for that business. For example, the high sales volume of the Mini car in the 1960s and 1970s was achieved at the wrong price and generated an insufficient gross profit margin. Great for sales staff's commission, but not so good for shareholders.

So the managers and directors, with their eye on the net profit margin, will have as a main concern the cash sum they receive after they have shipped the goods and sent the documentation to the discounter.

It would, however, be incorrect to say the exporter has no interest in the face value of the bill evidencing the sale and only in the net cash figure they receive. The face value of the bill will be of considerable concern to the importer who in due course has to meet the bill. If the exporter fails to focus on their clients' concerns, particularly price, this may very well lead to them losing the sale.

The exporter may start from the discounted net cash sum they will receive on the sale and then calculates the face value using whatever method and discount rate they are familiar with or are advised to use.

To regard the discount rate as the sole variable would be to attach little importance to the method of discounting and, as the examples in this chapter indicate, the price received by the exporter in the example at a discount rate of 12% per annum can vary between £6400 and £7352 depending on the method used.

The arbitrage opportunities that exist with these varieties of methods to value negotiable paper however are limited by both the imperfect nature of the secondary market and the risks associated with this type of financial trade instrument.

The Appendix considers approaches to calculating interest and discount rates and the importance of using derived yield curves for discounting zero coupon paper.

FIVE
The discount rate and interest rate risk

5.1 Introduction
5.2 The cost of funds element in the discount rate
5.3 The interest rate risk
5.4 Floating rate promissory notes
5.5 Methods of converting fixed rate to floating rate notes

5.1 Introduction

The semi-annual discount to yield is the most common discounting method used in forfaiting. In practice the method used will be the one that is most appropriate to the participants and their transaction needs. However, for simplicity, in the next three chapters and in order to make the discount method a constant, I will use the annual discount to yield method.

There are three factors that need to be taken into account in fixing the current market price (present value, PV) of a promissory note.

❏ **The face value of the note at maturity.** The face value of a note at maturity is fixed and is therefore constant.
❏ **The method of discounting.** For the purposes of this chapter, the only method of discounting used will be the annual discount to yield method with no days of grace.
❏ **The discount rate.** In this chapter the PV of the note will vary as a function of the discount rate. The discount rate is a combination of the estimated cost of funds for the period of the note plus a margin for the credit risk.

5.2 The cost of funds element in the discount rate

If a note has two years to run to maturity then the usual form would be to establish the two-year pure interest rate. Often the reference point will be the relevant London Interbank Offered Rate (LIBOR), although any credible objective rate specific to that currency and acceptable to the parties involved in the deal could be used.

The point may also be usefully made here that notes are often bought and sold in series. In the example below there are four notes A, B, C, D payable at six-monthly intervals over the next 24 months.

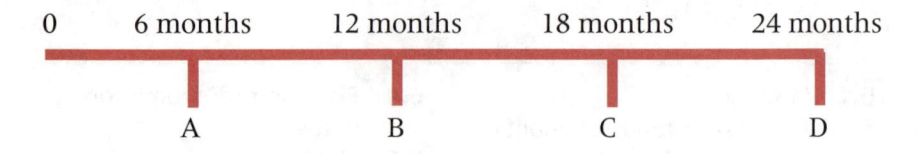

```
0        6 months      12 months      18 months     24 months
|------------|-------------|-------------|-------------|
             A             B             C             D
```

Each note may be sold independently of the others or together as a series. If they are sold individually, the cost of funds will be the rate based on the specific time period relevant to that note. If, however, they are sold as a series the cost of funds may be calculated on each note or the average life for the series will be used as the cost of funds for all the notes.

The average life of the series of four notes in the example using this yield curve as at time zero will be 15 months, each note having the same maturity face value.

	Note	Period to due date (months)
	A	6
	B	12
	C	18
	D	24
Sum	Four notes	60

Average life = months/notes = 60/4 = 15 months.

Using the cost of funds yield curve in Figure 5.1, the method used in the forfaiting market to establish the mid-market price for funds for 15 months would be 8.5%.

Calculating the average cost of funds is not an exact science; the longer the period the less accurate we can be. However, most traders

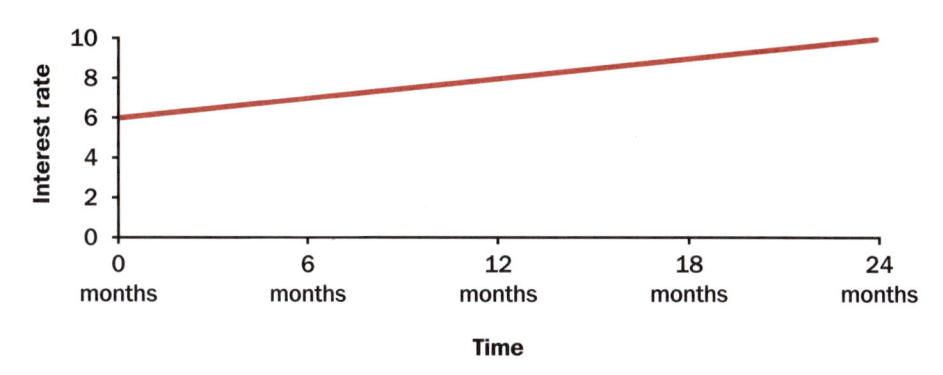

Figure 5.1 Monetary cost of funds yield curve.

will try to establish an objective cost of funds reference point (such as a specific bank LIBOR at an agreed point in time) and then put a credit margin on top of that figure to reach the aggregate discount rate to be used in the PV calculation.

We should now consider the fixed rate nature of this financial instrument and the possible attendant interest rate risk which is a result of the tenor of the asset not being matched by the tenor of the liability by the holder of the note.

However, one further caveat: the characteristic, in fact a major feature of without-recourse financing, is its free-market flexibility. Although most negotiable trade financial instruments are fixed rate instruments, if the market wants a floating rate note then such a variant on the fixed rate plain vanilla note will be evolved. Section 5.5 considers floating rate structures for medium-term fixed rate non-recourse financing.

5.3 The interest rate risk

In this example, there is an underlying trade of Italian machine exports (exporter) to a Czech furniture company (importer). At time zero (0), company Y (Y Co.), an investor in trade instruments, buys a single promissory note without recourse from the Italian machinery company (exporter), with a face value of 10,000 payable in three years' time by the Czech importer, guaranteed by the guarantor bank (Bank CZ) (see Figure 5.2).

The discount rate is 10% and the annual discount to yield is the method of discounting used. There is no commitment fee to be paid or days of grace.

44 Forfaiting for exporters

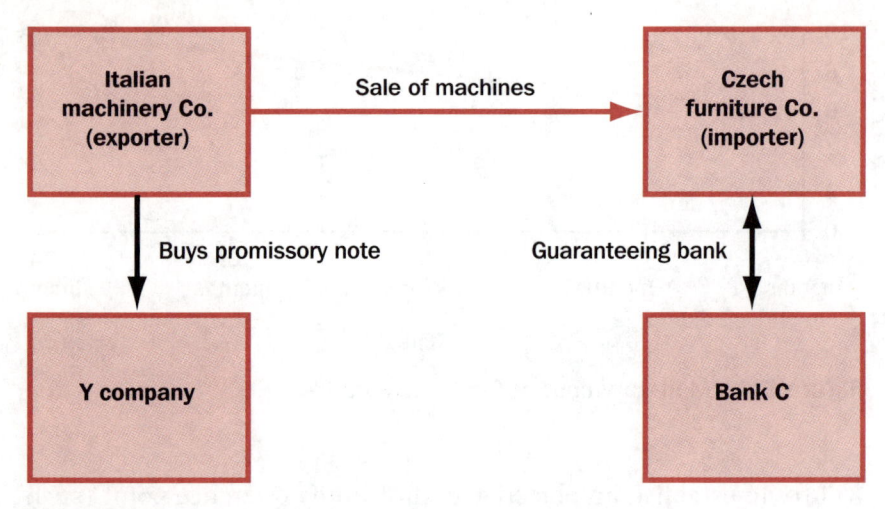

Figure 5.2 The underlying trade credit transaction.

The price paid by Y Co. to the exporter is

$$\text{NPV} = \frac{10{,}000}{(1.10)\,(1.10)\,(1.10)} = 7513$$

This is Y Co.'s sole asset (A). Y Co. has no equity (E) and therefore being debt financed has to borrow the funds (L) to purchase the asset. So at time zero, Y Co.'s balance sheet would be

$$\text{at time zero} \quad A = L + E$$

$$7513 = 7513 + 0$$

The asset (A) generates a fixed revenue stream at 10% per annum so that at the end of each period (one year), using the compound interest rate formula $P = A(1 + r)^n$ the PV of the asset will be, respectively

PV   *Change in asset value in period*

	Asset value		=	gross revenue
At time zero	7513	0 − 0	=	0
End of period one	8264	8264 − 7513	=	751
End of period two	9090	9090 − 8264	=	826
End of period three	10000	10000 − 9090	=	910

The discount rate and interest rate risk

At the end of each period we can calculate both the asset value and the gross revenue stream for that period. At the end of period one, before adjusting the liabilities for the expenses for the period, Y Co.'s balance sheet ($A = L + E$) and profit and loss account (revenue − expenses) will be

$$A = L + E + (\text{revenue} - \text{expenses})$$

End of period one   8264 =   (751   −   )

At time zero, Y Co. must decide how it will fund the asset purchase. The cost of the funding (expenses) is, for the purposes of the example, the sole expense of Y Co. and is not paid in cash but is rolled up. When Y Co. decides on the funding policy and its expense it may be in a position to calculate the liability due at each point in time and the expense over each period of time, assuming that the note will be met on due date and also that revenue and cost streams are apportioned equally across accounting periods. (Accounting allocation issues are considered in Chapter 9.)

Funding policies

Case 1. Y Co. obtains three-year funds with the interest due payable at the end of the three years, at an annual compound interest rate of 8%. Y Co. can now calculate its balance sheet and net profit (revenue − expenses) attributable to the equity share holders, at the end of and for each period. Assuming no taxation or dividend.

	Balance sheet						Profit and loss account
	A	=	L	+	E +	(rev. − exp)
At time zero	7513	=	7513	+	0	(0 − 0)
End of period one	8264	=	8114	+	150	(751 − 601)
End of period two	9090	=	8763	+	327	(826 − 649)
End of period three	10000	=	9464	+	536	(910 − 701)

With the Case 1 assumptions both the asset and liability tenors are matched and there is no interest rate risk.

Case 2. Keeping everything else constant let us now assume at time zero Y Co. faces a funding yield curve as shown in Figure 5.3.

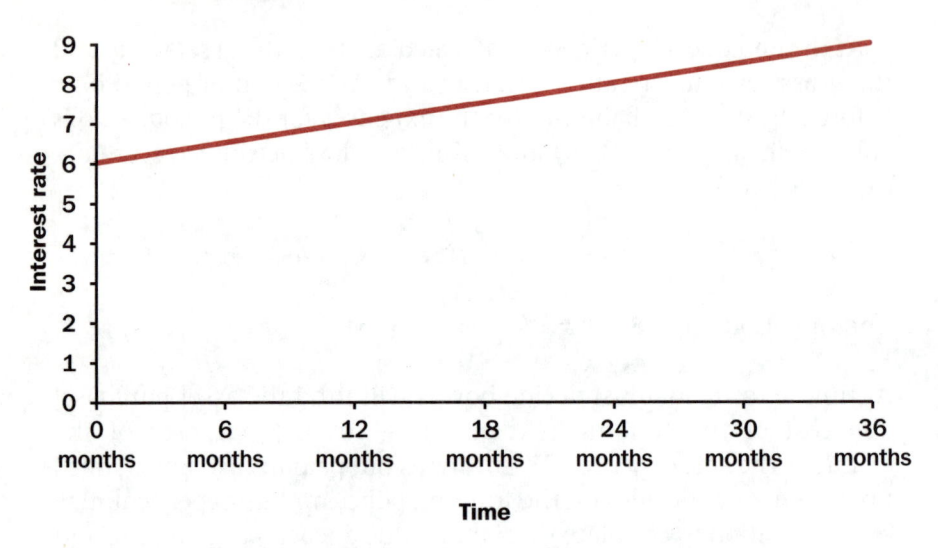

Figure 5.3 Funding yield curve facing Y Co. at time zero.

If Y Co. can obtain funding (either directly or by hedging the risk, see Figure 5.4) for three years (36 months) at 9% it can lock into a certain profit. Or it can obtain funds for a lesser period at a lower rate of interest. If Y Co. decides to fund for a shorter period than three years then at the date of refinancing Y Co. may be facing a yield curve that has changed substantially in shape and character. This may generate either windfall profits or losses for Y Co.'s shareholders. However, what is for certain is that with a fixed discount rate and mismatched funding Y Co. has an interest rate risk.

5.4 Floating rate promissory notes

Once the exporter has exchanged documents for cash, then for the exporter the consequent funding of the discounted promissory note and the interest rate risk carried by the holder of the note is of no commercial significance. The exporter has received the cash against the documentation and also, even in the event of the note not being paid, there is no recourse to the exporter. With forfaiting, in the event of non-payment at maturity the holder of the negotiable instrument has no right or recourse to the exporter or any previous holder(s).

However, even assuming the negotiable instrument is met at maturity, the successive holder(s) of the note to maturity, depending on their funding policy, may well run an interest rate risk. This may be out of choice or because the holder(s) are unable to obtain matching term funds. If the holder cannot obtain funding to match the tenor of the loan, then there are a number of ways to reduce or limit the interest rate risk.

Y Co. has a fixed rate asset funded short. If interest rates decrease, the capital value of the asset and the net revenue potential will rise. If interest rates increase the opposite will happen.

To fix the return and the capital value of the fixed rate asset at the intersect of the *X* and *Y* axes in Figure 5.4, Y Co. could buy a derivative financial instrument that would lock them into the position at the intersect. The financial instrument would act in the opposite direction to the underlying asset in the event of any changes in interest rates. This can be achieved with varying degrees of effectiveness through swaps, forwards or futures. Each of these hedging instruments imposes an obligation on the company. Y Co. could also buy an option against interest rate movements, which confers a certain cost on the company (the option premium), but the right and not an obligation to exercise that option if they wish to do so.

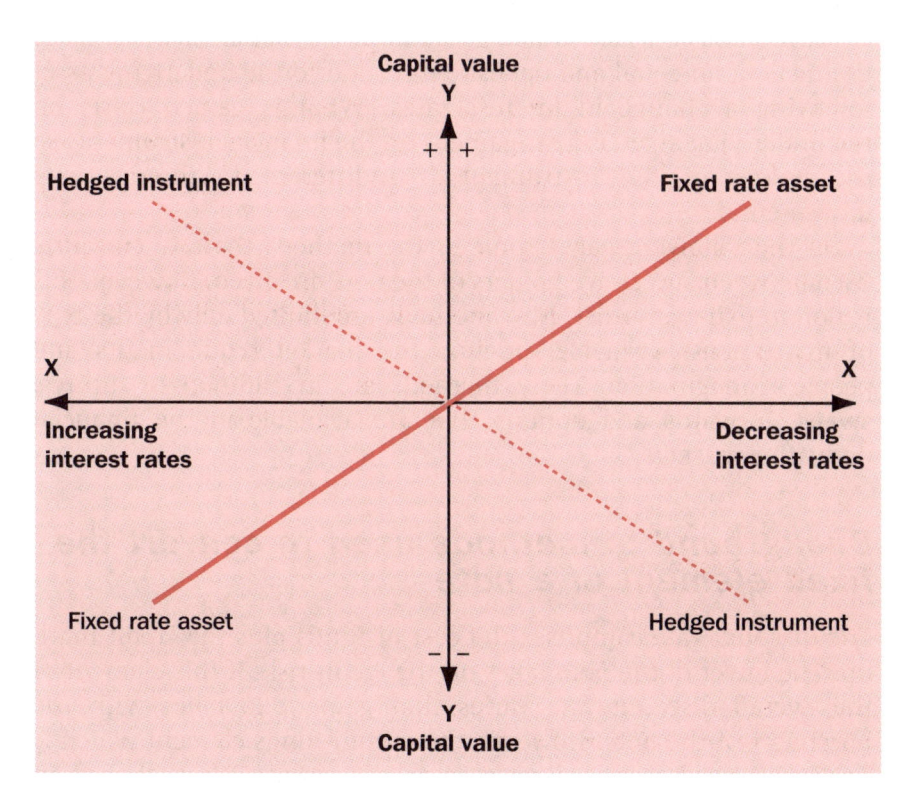

Figure 5.4 Hedging the fixed rate asset.

48   Forfaiting for exporters

5.5 Methods of converting fixed rate to floating rate notes

Medium-term without-recourse trade-related paper has characteristics similar to zero coupon bonds, in that there is no coupon or cash associated with either instrument until their maturity date. The standard version of both offers a fixed yield to maturity.

As mentioned earlier, this fixed interest characteristic and its attendant interest rate risk when the note is funded short is a matter of concern only to the holder of the note and not the exporter. However, it is possible that if the exporter of the underlying trade doesn't need cash, the exporter may choose to be the holder of the notes rather than discounting them. The exporter may prefer, as in the example in Section 5.4, to have 10,000 in three years' time rather than 7513 now.

How can the holder convert the fixed rate nature of the instrument into a floating rate instrument?

There are a number of ways this can be achieved. The basis of most of the methods is as illustrated in Figure 5.4; to obtain an instrument that acts in an equal and opposite direction to the underlying asset following a change in interest rates. What is gained (lost) on the underlying asset, is lost (gained) on the financial instrument. So the holder of the instrument is indifferent to interest rate movements.

On the following pages some of the methods that are currently used between successive holders of the note are given. However, this is not an exhaustive list. New methods are limited only by the type of instruments available, pricing, the market requirements and people's imagination. These methods are in addition to futures, swaps, forwards and options that are available in the financial derivative markets.

Background to methods used to convert the fixed element of a note

The discount rate comprises the cost of funds plus the credit mark up. The buyer of the note takes on the credit risk. If this element of the overall discount rate varies that gain or loss lies with the purchaser of the note. However, the cost of funds element which is fixed will need to be adjusted to take account of any change in interest rates.

The discount rate and interest rate risk   49

10% total discount rate

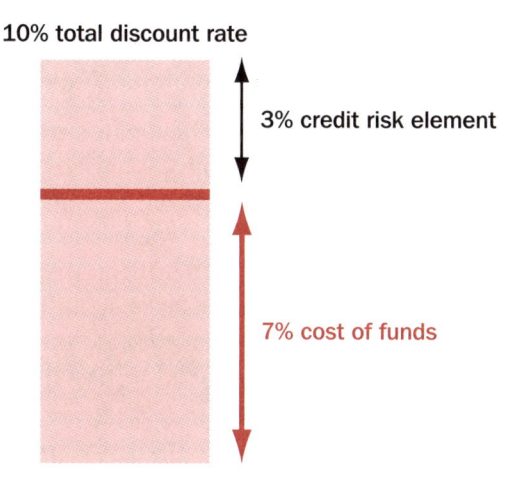

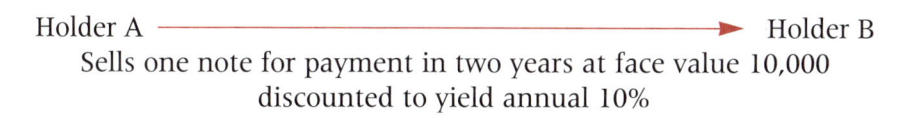

3% credit risk element

7% cost of funds

Holder A ———————————————→ Holder B
Sells one note for payment in two years at face value 10,000 discounted to yield annual 10%

Discount rate	Face value	NPV	Credit	Average cost
10%	10,000	8264	3%	7%

Using this information what could holder A offer to holder B to remove the interest rate risk to holder B, if B purchased the note? B could of course organize their own hedge through using the derivative/option market.

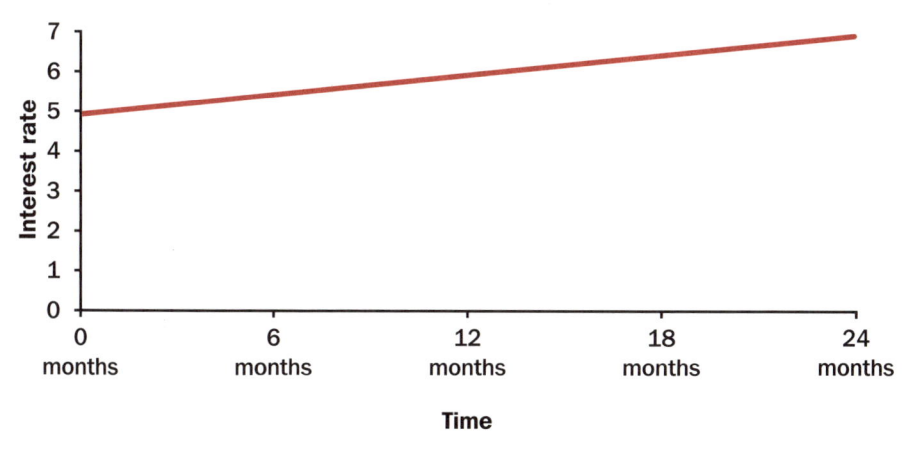

Figure 5.5 Yield curve facing holders A and B at time zero.

Methods used by holder A to change a fixed rate into a floating rate

❏ **Full payout method.** B pays the face value to A at time zero. A pays interest comprising LIBOR plus fixed credit margin on the outstanding face value. This method is not commonly used, although it is relatively simple to calculate. As it means A is borrowing from B the amount of the difference between B's face value payout to A and the calculated net payout figure. B may have credit concerns about A, A may have concerns about the cost of the enforced loan. Both will also need to fix on an agreed LIBOR tenor.

❏ **Capital payout method.** This method resolves the problem of enforced loans inherent in the full payout method. As in the secondary market, purchasers of the note may wish to pay the exact contracted amount received by the exporter from the importer – "the capital". This is a figure based on agreed rates between the importer and exporter, which may or may not be those rates used by two parties in the secondary market.

However, the underlying exporter/importer discount rates (cost of funds element) variance from the interest rates used by the two parties in the secondary market determine the interest make up payments between the two parties in the secondary market. As we move through time, as the outstanding capital element reduces so should the interest make up payments. This can lead to a multitude of adjustments based on notional rates and for this reason this method is not commonly used.

❏ **The industry standard method.** This is the most widely used method in the market, it first evolved in the early 1980s. This method, or near variants of it, particularly those evolved by Mark West at London Forfaiting Company, for changing a fixed into a floating rate instrument, are the industry standard between buyers and sellers in the secondary forfaiting market.

In the secondary market holder A sells a series of bills to B. They (A and B) would agree a nominal payout amount usually on a discount rate based on the average life cost of funds and an agreed credit margin and the face value of the bills. A capital value is then attributed to each note such that if there are no interest rate movements during the life of the bills, there will be no need for interest payments between A and B. The interest rate risk remains with A. A can run the interest rate risk or swap it, or buy futures, forwards or options to offset the interest rate risk. However, the credit risk is now with holder B; this risk is considered and evaluated in the next chapter.

The example below illustrates how to turn a fixed rate deal into a floating rate deal, which is not dissimilar to the mechanics of a simple interest rate swap.

Turning a fixed rate deal into a floating rate deal. An illustration

The following example illustrates the structure with which B may purchase from A a forfaiting transaction on a floating rate basis in the secondary market.

Terms and conditions

Total amount	US$4,000,000
Evidenced by	four promissory notes
Maturities	US$1,000,000 due 15/11/95
	US$1,000,000 due 15/05/96
	US$1,000,000 due 15/11/96
	US$1,000,000 due 15/05/97
Value date	15/05/95
Terms	six-month US$ LIBOR plus 1.5% per annum margin (365/360) on a floating basis payable in arrears.
	LIBOR to be fixed two business days prior to each period.

Floating rate structure
- **Step 1.** The transaction may be treated as a "fixed rate loan" whereby there are capital instalments yielding interest at a fixed rate of average life LIBOR plus margin.
- **Step 2.** The "fixed rate loan" is then converted to a "floating rate loan".

Step 1. "Fixed rate loan"

In order to achieve a "fixed rate loan" structure it is assumed that each promissory note is represented by a principal repayment element and an interest element which total to the face value of the promissory note. This is calculated by discounting the aggregate cash flow to their respective PV. Both A and B need to be in agreement on the discounting method used. These figures as illustrated in the "fixed rate loan" maturity schedule, are usually generated by A and then agreed by B.

The sum of all principal repayment amounts outstanding is called the outstanding principal. The outstanding principal also represents the amount that is payable at value date. Interest is calculated on the outstanding principal amount at a fixed rate (average life LIBOR plus margin) for the relevant number of days. The complete maturity schedule for the "fixed rate loan" is as follows:

"Fixed rate loan" maturity schedule

Maturity	Days	Principal repayment	Principal outstanding	Interest at 8.5%
15/11/95	184	843,496.13	3,602,390.89	156,503.87
15/05/96	182	881,144.16	2,758,894.76	118,555.84
15/11/96	184	918,435.20	1,877,450.60	81,564.80
15/05/97	181	959,015.41	959,015.41	40,984.59

A and B agree that the average life US$ LIBOR is 7.0%. This means that for the first period of 184 days, B will be earning interest at 8.5% per annum (including the 1.5% credit margin) on the outstanding principal of US$3,602,390.89, as follows:

❏ First period: 184 days – from value date (15/05/95) until the next principal repayment date (15/11/95).
❏ Interest: the principal outstanding from the beginning of the first period

US$3,602,390.89 × 8.5% × (184/360) = US$156,503.87.

❏ Payment: B will receive on 15/11/95 a note to an aggregate value of US$1,000,000.00. This is made up of a principal repayment of 843,496.13 and an interest element of 156,503.87.
❏ Each note: B will receive 1,000,000.00 at each maturity date made up of a principal repayment and interest based on a rate of 8.5% per annum.

Step 2. From "fixed rate loan" to "floating rate loan"

In converting the "fixed rate loan" previously described, to a structure whereby B receives interest on a floating basis at six-month US$ LIBOR + margin, there are three possible outcomes. These are subject to the caveat that A is in a position to support this swap over the course of its life.

❑ Outcome 1: the six-month US$ LIBOR + margin rate is the *same* as the average life US$ LIBOR + margin rate. There is no need for any payments from either A or B.
❑ Outcome 2: the six-month US$ LIBOR + margin rate is *lower* than the average life US$ LIBOR + margin rate. Then B will need to make up the interest rate differential to A.
❑ Outcome 3: the six-month US$ LIBOR + margin rate is *higher* than the average life US$ LIBOR + margin rate. Then A will need to make up the interest rate differential to B. Using the figures from the example the exact payment would be calculated as described below.

A and B agree that for the first period the six-month US$ LIBOR rate is 8.0%, *higher* than the average life US$ LIBOR of 7.0%. This means that for the first period B will be earning interest at 9.5% per annum (including the 1.5% margin) on the outstanding principal of US$3,602,390.89.

Interest at 9.5% per annum for the first period is calculated as follows:

❑ First period: 184 days from value date (15/05/95) until the next principal repayment date (15/11/95)
❑ Interest: the principal outstanding from the beginning of the first period: US$3,602,390.89 × 9.5% × (184/360) = US$174,916.09.
❑ Payment: B will receive on 15/11/95 a note to an aggregate value of US$1,000,000.00. This is made up of a principal repayment of 843,496.13 and an interest element of 156,503.87. B will also receive the interest rate differential from A of 18,412.22. Which is the difference between 174,916.09 and 156,503.87.
❑ Each following note: B will receive 1,000,000.00 at each maturity date made up of an interest and a principal repayment element based on a rate of 8.5% per annum from the obligor and in addition a net amount due to or from A, which converts the negotiable instrument from being a fixed rate to a floating rate instrument.

SIX
Credit risk

6.1	Introduction	6.4	The country risk
6.2	The exporter	6.5	The bank guarantee credit risk
6.3	The current holder		

6.1 Introduction

Credit judgement is the cornerstone of successfully holding or trading non-recourse trade-related negotiable instruments. Credit risk is dynamic and has to be addressed on a continuing basis by the holders of the instrument. However, the credit margin is a fixed element in the discount rate when the credit is originally arranged for the underlying trade deal.

If the holder of the negotiable instrument runs an interest rate risk by funding the asset short during a period of falling interest rates the holder will make windfall profits. During a period of rising interest rates those net profits will be reduced and may in due course become holding losses. Initially the holder may (mistakenly) regard the credit margin as a shock absorber against rising interest rates. But as shown in Chapter 5 the interest rate risk can be hedged. The credit margin element in the discount rate cannot be hedged. Get it wrong and it is not the return on the asset, but the return of the actual asset that becomes the major concern, with the potential of an ensuing capital loss and a consequent reduction in the company's equity.

Dynamic credit judgement is crucial. Such that the holder of the negotiable instrument has a high-debt return for a high-debt risk. Once the holder has a high-debt return for an equity risk, then over time the holder's equity base will be diminished.

6.2 The exporter

In Figure 6.1 the exporter (seller) has an underlying sales contract (1) with the importer (buyer). The exporter has also arranged credit terms (2) for the importer by making a forfaiting contract with forfaiter W. The importer (3) has arranged for a bank to guarantee the without recourse trade instruments.

The exporter (4) delivers the goods to the importer against documentation from the importer, which the exporter now holds. The exporter could hold the non-recourse bank-guaranteed trade instruments until maturity, but in this example discounts them with forfaiter W (5) under the terms and conditions of the previously agreed forfaiting contract. When the notes are discounted by forfaiter W, the exporter receives the cash from forfaiter W and has no credit risk or any contingent liability on their balance sheet. With forfaiting transactions, in this example, all the subsequent holders (6, 7, 8) (forfaiters X, Y, Z) have no recourse against previous holders or the exporter in the event of them holding the trade instrument at maturity and the instrument not being met on due date by the importer or the guarantor. The credit risk lies solely with the current holder, in this example forfaiter Z.

6.3 The current holder

In Figure 6.1 we can see that at maturity the credit risk will be with the current holder, forfaiter Z.

That risk will comprise two parts: (a) the country risk of the importer (b) the guaranteeing bank and importer or just the importer if there is no bank guarantee.

We are at a point in time, when forfaiter Z is holding the documentation, which consists of one promissory note evidencing the payment due under the underlying transaction between the importer and the exporter. The note is guaranteed by a bank (G Bank). Forfaiter Z has paid Y a payout value for the note and is expecting to receive, at the maturity of the note, the face value from G Bank. *In the event of non-payment Z has no recourse to the exporter, W, X or Y.*

What are the credit risks facing forfaiter Z?

Credit risk was previously classified into two major groupings: (a) the country risk and (b) the guaranteeing bank, or the importer if there is no bank guarantee.

Credit risk 57

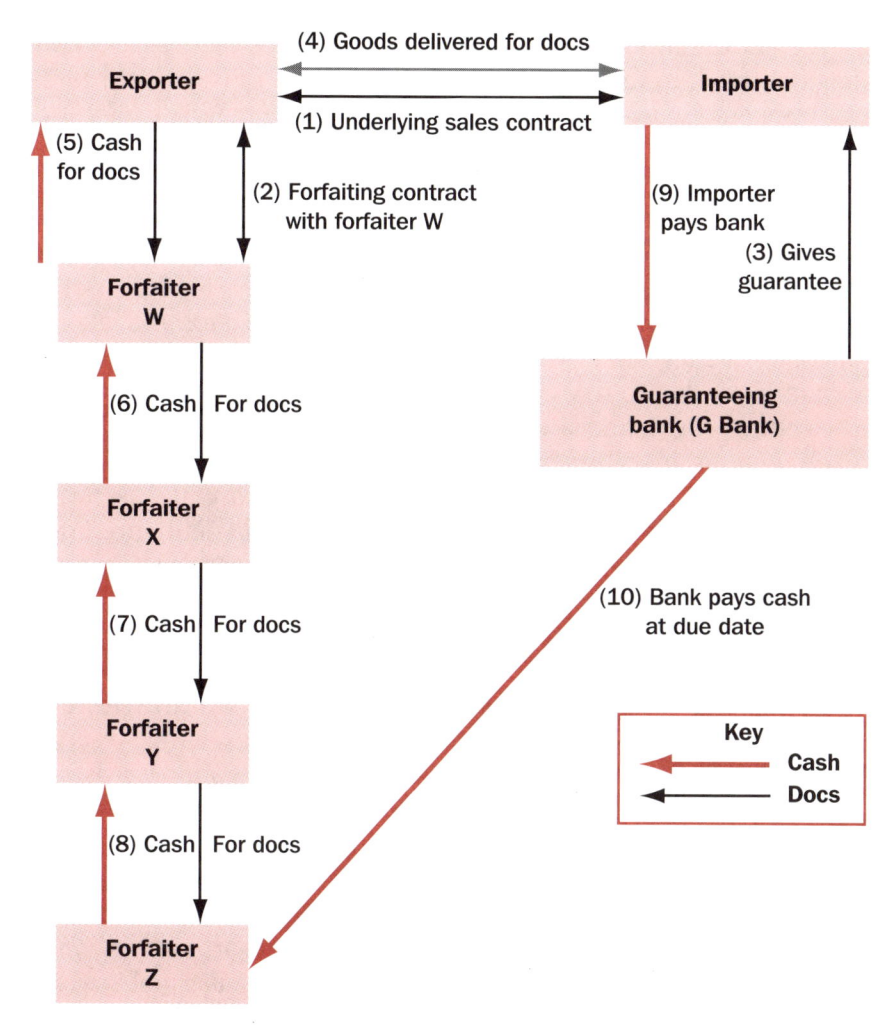

Figure 6.1 A forfaited structured deal.

6.4 The country risk

Economic, political and social conditions in the importer's country during the lifetime of the promissory note may alter such that the central bank/ministry of finance decide/decree/are forced to accept that foreign exchange is not available to meet foreign indebtedness. Or that it should be allocated in a certain manner. Perhaps, only to meet trade obligations and not capital repayments on syndicated loans, or to allocate repayment according to the domestic standing/ownership of the guaranteeing bank, or the standing of the lending institution.

The permutations are many and varied. It is possible that G Bank has the funds to meet the bill, but those funds must be paid to the central bank to be distributed according to some maturity allocation schedule.

How can forfaiter Z assess this country risk?

This risk, particularly if a country has limited hard currency reserves, needs to be considered daily. An evolving view needs to be taken and that view adjusted accordingly. To set country limits annually and review them periodically or on a *post hoc* calamity basis, is better than nothing, but clearly doesn't address the dynamics of day-to-day changes. Analysts for forfaiter Z by visiting the country, the banks and analysing the central bank's role and its likely actions in different situations and deciphering the central bank's formal and informal attitude to the ranking and tiering of trade debt, bonds and syndicated loans, can enhance their judgement in assessing country risk. This can be expanded by tapping into formalized databases through a variety of platforms and terminals. This is all part of the analysts' information assimilation process.

Hunch and feel make assessing sovereign risk an art. However, hunch without an analysis of the level of foreign exchange reserves, reports on the country's payment record, the trends and forecasts for the country's trading relations with the outside world can become merely a subjective value judgement without substance.

Many, if not all, international finance houses, banks and trading companies have an annual due diligence country limit assessment process. This in-house process, always an integral part of country risk assessment, can be, enhanced by visits and a biannual or even monthly reviews and not solely on a reactive crisis basis.

Country risk analysis isn't just about the possibility of outright default or the possibility of rescheduling. It is also about the real or anticipated changes and their interpretation in the relative standings of countries and regions. The recent growth in technology has resulted in previously unavailable databases being readily and cheaply accessible and this information is quickly transmitted to secondary market prices even in a relatively imperfect market such as the secondary à forfait market.

The question to be resolved by forfaiter Z is: does the importing country have, or more importantly will it have the liquidity in foreign exchange as at the note's maturity date to allow G Bank to meet the outstanding debt? Furthermore, even if the country via

G Bank has the hard currency, is the central monetary authority likely to have the willingness or the intention of releasing those funds?

The answer to these questions will be reflected in the credit risk element of the discount rate used in evaluating the present value (PV) of the note.

6.5 The bank guarantee credit risk

Although most forfaiting notes are guaranteed by a commercial bank in the importer's country, it can be the case that the importer is of sufficient credit standing (perhaps, for example, the importer is a government entity or agency) that there may be no need for the avalization of the note by a bank. The perception of a bank guaranteed note is that the bank guarantee enhances both the credit standing of the note and its tradability in the secondary market. Most forfaiting transactions are bank guaranteed. The importer will pay a guarantee fee directly to the bank for this facility. This fee is usually paid, in advance, as a percentage of the face value of the note(s) for the period of the debt. Banks in countries where liquidity in foreign currency is often in short supply can generate off-balance sheet revenue by guaranteeing the corporate risk. Where there is considerable liquidity in foreign currency, the bank which has ready access to that liquidity may prefer to enhance its revenue potential by making a direct loan to the importer rather than adding its guarantee. In these circumstances forfaiting may not be the most efficient method of importer financing.

However, in Figure 6.1 "the structured deal" forfaiter Z's promissory note is guaranteed by G Bank. The credit weighting attached to G Bank will comprise a crucial element of the aggregate credit risk in the discount rate.

All forfaiting analysts will have a view on each bank's credit standing whose guarantee they are prepared to consider and rely on, for face value repayment of a promissory note.

Bank credit analysis departments will have access to a variety of data and in-house systems for analysis of other banks. Published data will be augmented by bank analysts visiting other banks, analysing their figures and estimating future problems and opportunities that may face the guaranteeing bank. They will then identify the current credit margin element that is appropriate to that bank.

Summary

The credit risk element of the discount rate is an amalgam of the existing and potential country risk and the bank (or corporate) risk. However, it will also be a function of the forfaiter's current book, the trader's market knowledge and experience, the size of the note and its tenor, the counterparties and the ability to sell the deal on. However, we must not confuse the roles of the forfait trader and the credit analyst:

❑ The forfait trader's primary concern is buy low and sell high.

❑ The credit analyst's primary concern is: if the note is purchased will the guarantor be in a position to meet the note on due date and will the importer's country have access to foreign currency for the guarantor to be able to make the payment and further will the authorities allow that payment to be made?

Exporter rate and tenor information

Most forfaiting houses, each with its own distinctive style, will periodically issue booklets or updated sheets indicating the countries and the periods which they will consider discounting forfaiting transactions. This indicative information will become quickly dated, but is a useful source of information for the exporter and potential exporter.

SEVEN
Documentation and documentation risk

7.1 Documentation risk
7.2 Transport documentation
7.3 Financial instruments evidencing the debt
7.4 Types of documentation
7.5 How the risk on documentation can be covered: avals, guarantees, burgschafts, (stand by) deferred payment letters of credit
7.6 Contingent liabilities
7.7 Transaction, payout and other documentation risks

7.1 Documentation risk

Credit risk (Chapter 5) and interest rate risk (Chapter 6), with regard to non-recourse financing or any other form of credit, are usually difficult to evaluate but relatively easy to identify. Both of these types of risk are familiar to financial institutions and there is an industry which advises on the assessment and mitigation of these types of risk. Documentation risk, which can be further subdivided into specific types, is a practical concern that must not be understated. It is a very real risk. However, before exploring this risk in detail, it may be useful to consider three fundamental points which need to be addressed between the forfaiter and the exporter in order to minimize this risk.

1 The exact price of the goods and the interest to be charged to the buyer, if any, must be established. To say, for example, that the overall invoiced amount is the retail price plus a charge for interest at LIBOR plus 2%, is in practical terms not sufficient. At the time

of purchasing the transaction, the forfaiter will need to know the exact date and time of a specific reference bank's LIBOR. This will present no great problem to either the forfaiter or the exporter but there needs to be an exactly specified and agreed invoiced (cost and interest) amount.

2 The exact maturity of the payments by the buyer must be established. An ordinary forfaiting deal is closed before the known shipment date. The payment of discount proceeds can only be paid to the exporter once the shipment date has been established and consequently maturity dates are certain.

3 The forfaiter will also require a simple documentary transfer mechanism that is acceptable to the secondary market. The most appropriate simple transfer payment mechanism is generally held to be a promissory note or bill of exchange, issued or accepted by the buyer and then avalized by a bank in the importer's country, that is acceptable to the secondary market. Such documentation may be transferred by a simple "without recourse" endorsement.

The variety of trade finance payment mechanisms gives forfaiting an enhanced flexibility. The way in which forfaiting payment mechanisms have been grafted on to established trade documentation gives forfaiting a market acceptability. However it is the variety of potential documentation which contributes to the documentary risk. In order to appreciate this risk, it seems appropriate to consider initially documentation and documentary credits as a whole.

In Figure 7.1 – a forfaited structured deal – used in Chapter 6 and shown again here, there will be documentation associated with

A The underlying contract of sale between the exporter and importer.
B The transport and supporting documentation on the physical despatch of the goods sold.
C The payment and credit conditions for the goods sold, which is part of item (1), the underlying contract of sale, between the exporter and the importer.
D The forfaiting contract documentation between the exporter and forfaiter.
E The documentation on payout to the holder at maturity.

There are many practitioners and many excellent books (see the Bibliography at the end of this chapter) based on a wealth of national and international legal precedent on contract law in all countries that

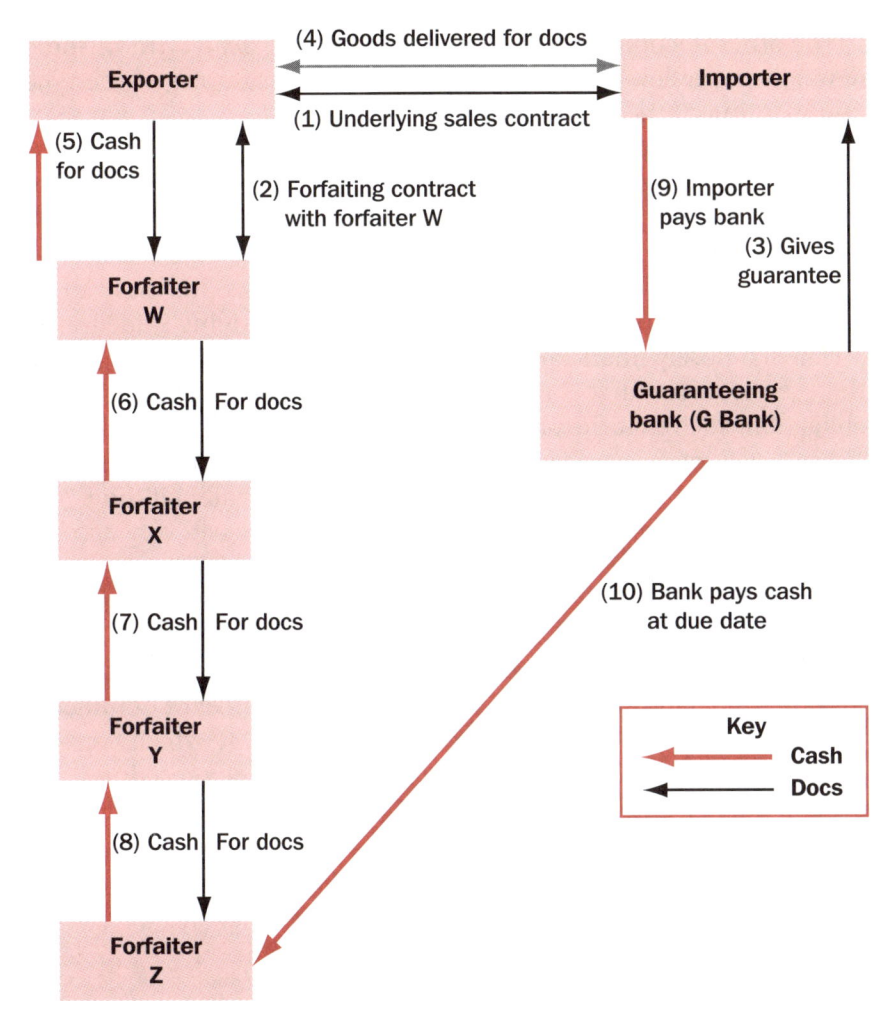

Figure 7.1 A forfaited structured deal.

trade nationally and internationally. It is sufficient for the purposes of this book to restate that the forfaiting contract abstracts itself absolutely from (**A**) the underlying sales contract.

Section 7.2 deals briefly with the (**B**) transport documentation. Although the forfaiting contract also abstracts itself from this element of the sales contract, the shipping documentation (e.g. the date of the bill of lading) will, however, probably provide a trigger in the forfaiting agreement.

64   *Forfaiting for exporters*

The other documentation points (**C, D, E**) are dealt with in some detail in the following sections giving specific examples of the type and wording of the documents used.

There are two caveats.

First, non-recourse negotiable instruments have historically been used to evidence an underlying trade receivable. However, the same negotiable instruments can also evidence a purely financial obligation. The documentation and the associated risks are likely to be different depending whether it evidences an underlying trade transaction or a purely financial obligation. For the moment let us assume that the non-recourse instrument evidences an underlying trade obligation, such that the physical trade is for "cash later documents". These "cash later documents" must be correct, valid and authorized by all parties to the underlying transaction and legally binding.

Second, documentation and statutory precedents will vary according to the legal jurisdiction of the trading countries, as may the associated documentation risks. Most countries do have their own well-established laws on bills of exchange, which are not radically dissimilar. In cases where we are dealing with letters of credit almost all countries are happy to apply the International Chamber of Commerce (ICC) Uniform Customs & Practices No. 500 (1993) which contain globally accepted methods and documentary credit procedures. As from 1 January 1996 the new ICC Uniform Rules for Collections (URC522) and the ICC Uniform Rules for bank to bank reimbursements under documentary credits (URR525) have been implemented.

7.2   Transport documentation

Let's take an example as illustrated in Figure 7.2. There are two well-established companies that have been trading with each other for many years. X Co. is exporting tractors to M Co. The companies have an open account such that X Co. will invoice M Co. on despatch of the tractors from X Co.'s factory and M Co. will pay the invoice on

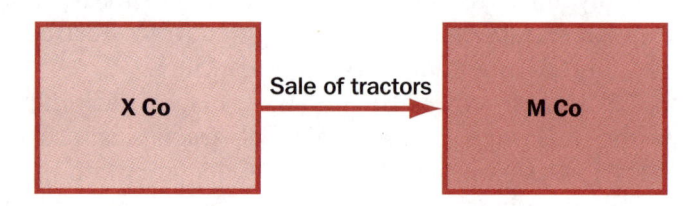

Figure 7.2   Open account operations.

arrival of the tractors at M Co.'s factory. This type of sale is usually referred to as an open account operation.

X Co. will organize a contract with a shipper (who will issue a bill of lading on delivery of the tractors to the shipper) and X Co. will send the original bills of lading to M Co. together with the invoice. On arrival of the tractors M Co. will present the original bill of lading to the shipper and collect the tractors. M Co. then pays the invoice. In this example there is no need for external credit since M Co. and X Co. operate an open account.

The transport documentation is concerned with the physical goods, the cost of freight and the ownership at specific points in time. Each of these points needs to be agreed and identified and the transport documentation exists to do just that. There are well-established legal and physical precedents to protect all parties to the trade. Forfaiters should be aware of transport documentation but it is something they abstract themselves from, as they do from the underlying sales contract. The forfaiters sole direct concern is the payment due under the sales contract.

In Figure 7.2 the exporter invoices the importer directly, as is the case in most business transactions within national/legal trading regions. However, if an international trade transaction involves time, distance and credit uncertainty, then the buyer and seller may want certain safeguards against the possible non-beneficial actions or performance of the other party, irrespective of whether the exporter (the supplier) is giving a deferred payment period (credit) to the importer or requires immediate payment (sight).

7.3 Financial instruments evidencing the debt

Payment in advance – the seller's preferred route – or confirmed, irrevocable documentary credits payable on sight have developed to address the payment obligations of the buyer and the actual or potential concerns of the seller. A further element of financial trade instruments has been the credit element sometimes extended (at a price) to the buyer, as either a supplier credit or since the 1970s as a buyer credit.

The financial instruments used are (see Section 7.4):

- promissory notes
- bills of exchange
- book receivables.

66   *Forfaiting for exporters*

These evidence the underlying trade and the ensuing obligation by the importer and are legally enforceable negotiable trade receivables and can be covered by (see Section 7.5):

- avalization
- guarantees
- burgschaft
- letters of credit-deferred/sight (including stand by)
- confirmations (full and silent).

A summary may be of some use here to detail the range of possible payment conditions in the export sales contract between the exporter and importer. The objective of the summary shown in Figure 7.3 is to put the forfait transaction within an overall structure of payment conditions.

Prepayment is not listed in Figure 7.3, but from the exporter's point of view to have both the cash and the goods is probably from the exporter's perspective the most risk averse position.

In Figure 7.3, along the horizontal, are listed:

- **Payment at sight.** From the exporter's view, transfer of ownership of the goods is at the same point in time as the exchange in value for those goods.
- **Supplier credit.** This is where the exporter gives credit to the buyer when the underlying importer payment obligation is evidenced by a negotiable instrument and from our point of view the main area of interest. The agreement of a supplier credit in the export contract is the all important precondition for the use of a forfaiting sale at a later stage.

Contract terms	Payment at sight Cash Payment	Supplier credit Exporter gives credit
Possible documentation	A) Open account B) Collections C) Sight L/C's	1) Bill of exchange 2) Promissory notes 3) Book receivables 4) Deferred L/C's 5) Guarantees/Burgschaft

Figure 7.3 Payment conditions in the export contract.

Buyer credit is not listed in Figure 7.3. This is a more recent form of credit and is usually in the form of a loan or credit agreement between the exporter's bank and the importer's bank for the use of the importer.

Buyer credits were designed to be used with state-backed export credit agency guarantee (ECA, such as the ECGD in the UK, Coface in France, Hermes in Germany). At the time of writing, there have been a couple of examples where non-recourse obligations have been used in conjunction with buyer credit.

On the vertical in Figure 7.3 is listed for each of the above, with the exception of prepayment, the respective **contract terms** and **possible documentation**.

Before we consider types of documentation and how the risk on the documentation can be covered, it may be useful to restate the defining characteristic that differentiates forfait transactions from other types of supplier credit.

Subject to sovereign statute there are a variety of documentary credit instruments that can be used to evidence the underlying debt. These instruments are usually with recourse to previous holders and ultimately the drawer in the event of their non-payment on a due date by the obligor/guarantor. A forfaiting finance transaction can be evidenced by exactly the same range of financial instruments but they will be discounted, bought and sold without recourse to previous holders and the exporter in the event of their non-payment on due date by the obligor/guarantor.

7.4 Types of documentation

7.4.1 Bills of exchange

Bills of exchange (see Figure 7.4) are normally drawn by the exporter. X Co., the exporter, will issue a bill of exchange which is then accepted by the importer. The importer's bank can either add its aval (endorsement guaranteeing payment) to the bills of exchange or issue a separate letter of guarantee, to document their additional payment obligation. Bills of exchange can also be issued as a requirement of a letter of credit. For example, in Figure 7.6 the bill is issued by X Co. and accepted by the letter of credit opening bank, Bank M and is the payment method of the associated letter of credit. The bill of exchange results in the trade debt being far easier to discount on the primary or secondary market.

68   Forfaiting for exporters

[Bill of exchange template with fields: At/On, the order of, for value received pay against this bill of exchange to, the sum of, effective payment to be made in, without deduction for and free of any present or future taxes, impost, collection charges, levies or duties of any nature. This bill of exchange is payable at, Drawn on:, Per Aval for account of the drawee:, For Acceptance]

Exporter (X Co)

(beneficiary)
(drawer)
(issuer)

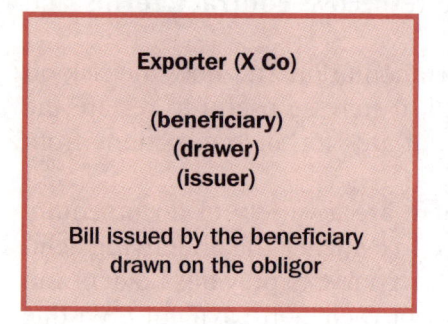

Bill issued by the beneficiary drawn on the obligor

Importer (M Co)

(obligor)
(drawee)
(acceptor)

Bill accepted by the obligor to the order of the beneficiary

Figure 7.4   Bills of exchange.

It is also, without being too trite, the case that irrespective of the mechanics used, the basic requirement of the forfaiting market is acceptable documentation and acceptable entities.

The beauty of a bill of exchange is its simple transferability mechanism. Laws on bills of exchange around the world cover the endorsement in its various forms as the means of transferring a bill of exchange to a further new *bona fide* holder. An endorsement by definition is the simple statement of the current *bona fide* holder (in the first place the exporter, X Co.) duly signed by them. In its pure form an endorsement is *with recourse*. In the example above in Figure 7.4 this means although the original holder has transferred all rights under the bill of exchange to another party this new *bona fide* holder may turn to the endorser X Co. for payment at maturity should the original drawee (obligor, M Co.) fail to make the payment at due date. Obviously the forfaiting market has to assure the exporter, X Co., especially that this right of recourse of future *bona fide* holders at maturity may not be used. To achieve this the currently used mechanism is simply to use *without recourse endorsements*. In practice this means that the words *without recourse* (or similar meanings in other languages such as *ohne Regress*, etc.) are added to the endorsement(s). By definition in many laws on bills of exchange this excludes the right of recourse of future *bona fide* holders to previous holders/endorsers.

It should be added that such simple mechanism of cancelling payment obligations does not exist for the recourse on drawers of bills of exchange. Article 9 of the International Convention for Commercial Bills (Geneva Conference 1930) states that although the drawer can release themselves from acceptance, the drawer cannot set aside their obligation as the drawer of the bill of exchange (as before, the drawer guarantees both acceptance and payment, though they may release themselves from guaranteeing acceptance, they cannot release themselves from guaranteeing payment). So bills of exchange issued by the exporter will always leave the exporter with a contingent liability. It should be noted by way of an aside that the UK was not a signatory to the Geneva Convention nor the United Nations Convention.

To minimize the exporter's residual risk as the issuer, as far as legally possible, the forfaiter may give a written undertaking to the issuer/exporter that if at maturity the bill is not met then the forfaiter and any future *bona fide* holder will take no action against the exporter. This is legally enforceable in certain countries under the law of contracts, and where it isn't at present, no precedent has been made by a forfaiter on non-payment at maturity against an unpaid bill where the forfaiter has attached a written undertaking.

For bills of exchange, although statutory differences exist, the usual form is that whereas successive traders of the bill of exchange may endorse without recourse they cannot waive the obligations of the drawer. However, I have detailed a sample of wording for a waiver that is currently used in the market:

> although it is not possible under the law on Bills of Exchange to exclude the right of recourse against the drawer, we hereby expressly confirm to waive any recourse against [*name of the exporter*]. This waiver shall be binding upon us and any successor in title.

Contents of a bill of exchange

Not all bills of exchange will conform to the example above either in style or content. So a detailed listing of the usual contents is summarized in Table 7.1.

Table 7.1 International bill of exchange (pro forma)

Place and date of issue	Currency and amount in figures
On [fixed date] for value received, pay against this bill of exchange	
to order of	[name of beneficiary]
the sum of	[amount in words]
effective payment to be made in	[type of currency]
without deduction for and free of any tax, impost, levy or duty present or future of any nature	[place]
This bill of exchange is payable at [signature of exporter]	[domicile]
Drawn on	[name and address of drawee/importer]
Accepted	[signature of drawee/importer]

7.4.2 Promissory notes

A promissory note (see Figure 7.5) is issued by the importer (obligor) and is a promise by the importer to pay the exporter (beneficiary). This is the preferable documentation for both the forfaiter and the secondary market and even more so for the exporter as (a) it has all the advantages of a bill of exchange with respect to the applicable strict laws; and (b) as the importer issues the document there is no contingent liability to the exporter on the note in the event that it is not met at maturity by the importer (issuer).

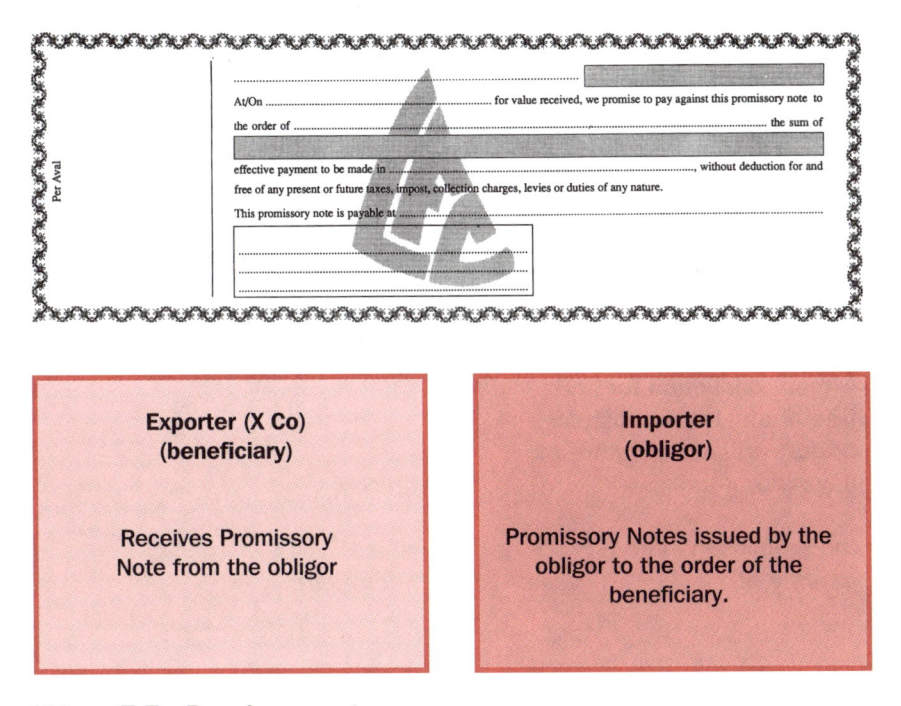

Exporter (X Co) (beneficiary)	Importer (obligor)
Receives Promissory Note from the obligor	Promissory Notes issued by the obligor to the order of the beneficiary.

Figure 7.5 Promissory notes.

Contents of a promissory note

Not all promissory notes will conform to the example above either in style or content. So a detailed listing of the usual contents has been summarized in Table 7.2.

Table 7.2 International promissory note (pro forma)

Place and date of issue	Currency and amount in figures
On	[fixed date]
for value received I/We	[name of issuer]
promise to pay against this promissory note to the to order of	[name of beneficiary]
the sum of	[amount in words]
effective payment to be made in	[type of currency]
without deduction for and free of any tax, impost, levy or duty present or future of any nature	[place]
the promissory note is payable at	[domicile]
signature of issuer	[signature]

7.4.3 Book receivables

Book receivables are an amount due to an exporter for goods sold, but as book receivables are not evidenced by a negotiable instrument, there is no negotiable instrument to be avalized. Consequently a separate letter of guarantee or letter of credit, in whatever form, has to be used.

Contents of a letter of guarantee

Not all guarantees conform either in style or content. So a detailed listing of the usual contents has been summarized in Table 7.3.

Table 7.3 Guarantee (pro forma)

For value received I/we hereby irrevocably and unconditionally guarantee payment on behalf of	[*name of importer*]
For the amount of	[*amount in words and figures*]
For which the following promissory notes, bills of exchange have been issued, (or book receivables allocated)	
Amounts	Maturities
To the order of	Issued by
If	[*name of exporter*]
does not pay for any reason whatsoever, I/we will pay at first demand even without the notes/bills having been protested.	
	[*name of guarantor*]
This guarantee is fully and freely transferable under written advice.	
	[*signature of guarantor*]

7.5 How the risk on documentation can be covered: avals, guarantees, burgschafts, (stand by) deferred payment letters of credit

The most favoured form of negotiable instrument for trading in the forfaiting secondary market is a promissory note, which is subject to less statutory precedent than a bill of exchange. To maximize its tradability, from the credit risk perspective, the promissory note should be avalized by a reputable bank. An aval is the additional, unconditional and irrevocable payment obligation of the importer's (avalizing) bank authorized by signature directly on the promissory note.

An aval is the preferred form of guarantee as it is self-evidently irrevocable and unconditional as long as the buyer's country's law does not impose specific restrictions. The word "aval" has come from the Geneva Conventions on Bills of Exchange of 1930 Articles 30, 31 and 32, being French for "guarantee". Article 31 says that the "aval" is expressed by the words "good as aval" (good for value). The United Nations Convention on Bills of Exchange of 9 December 1988, Article 46 uses the words "Guarantor" and "Guarantee", but goes on: "A Guarantee is expressed by the words 'guaranteed', 'aval', 'good as aval' or words of similar import ..." The word "avalorization" sometimes appears, which is an Anglo-Saxon corruption of the French word *aval*, which is according to the various conventions a guarantee. An aval however can be either, like a guarantee, not on the bill but as an allonge, or written on the bill or promissory note itself.

In some countries, such as the United States, at the time of writing, an aval is not a legally recognized form of security and a standby letter of credit is the generally preferred type of guarantee. A separate letter of guarantee can be in many cases as useful as an aval if it is unconditional, irrevocable, payable at first demand and easily transferable. There are many possible and acceptable wordings. Unfortunately there are no *standard* wordings so in each case a careful check has to be run. Less favourable are *Burgschaft(en)* an instrument almost exclusively used by the former Comecon countries. The word stems from a German legal definition which describes a form of guarantee which is *not* abstract but dependent on the satisfactory fulfilment of an underlying transaction. A burgschaft therefore will always contain phrases referring to the underlying transaction and it can only be made abstract after all obligations of the exporter, X Co., have been fulfilled to the full satisfaction of the importer, M Co. As the burgschaft issuing bank does not take any view itself when this point is reached but only reacts to the instructions of the importer, an exporting company may find itself with a useless guarantee if there is a dispute on the underlying contract. There seems to be no English language translation for this form of guarantee.

Letters of credit – deferred/sight (including stand by credits)

While obtaining bills of exchange or promissory notes covered by an aval or separate written guarantee is desirable from the exporter's point of view, it does raise potential problems for the importer, depending on the timing of the transfer of the documents to the exporter. Ideally, the exporter would like to obtain the documentation as soon as possible, prior to delivery but this would entail the importer providing abstract collateral for goods which they have not received. What if the documents are released but the goods are never delivered? In practice there are a number of ways in which both parties' requirements can be addressed and covered; for instance, a transfer of the payment documents against the documents of title (e.g. bills of lading), possibly under some form of trustee agreement.

However, the most common and perhaps the fairest alternative for both parties, is to have the payment obligation covered by a documentary letter of credit (L/C).

Whole textbooks have been written on the subject of L/Cs and anyone wishing to understand the characteristics and obligations of the L/Cs should certainly study the International Chamber of Commerce publication *The Uniform Customs and Practices for Documentary Credits*, 1993 Revision (UCP500).

Briefly, a L/C is a written payment obligation (almost always irrevocable) issued by the importer's bank (the L/C opening bank) to pay an amount of money to the beneficiary of the L/C (the exporter) against presentation by the beneficiary of predefined documents. The most common documents required under L/Cs are invoices, shipping/transport documents of title (e.g. bills of lading/airway bills), packing lists, certificates of origin and insurance certificates. The documents submitted must conform exactly to the terms set out in the L/C and it is the exporter's responsibility to ensure that credit-

76 Forfaiting for exporters

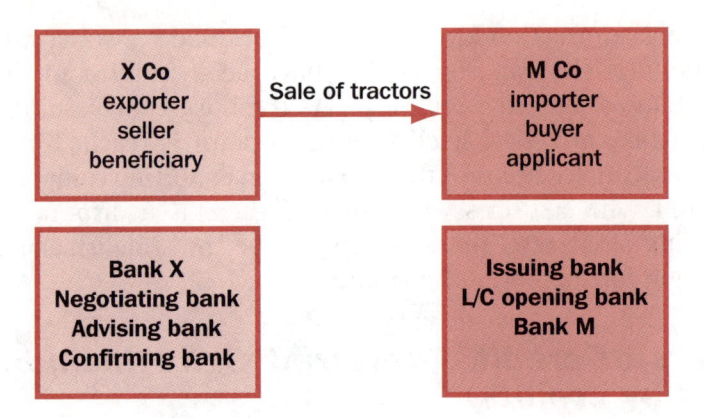

Figure 7.6 Letters of credit.

conforming documents are presented. Any discrepancies may result in non-payment.

L/Cs are normally advised to a beneficiary by a bank located in the beneficiary's country (the L/C advising bank) – usually either the issuing bank's correspondent bank or the exporter's house bank.

Payment under an irrevocable (but unconfirmed, see below) L/C is often dependent on the acceptance of the predefined documents set out in the terms of the L/C (credit-conforming documents) by the L/C opening bank. However, some L/Cs do authorize the advising bank to check that the documents conform to the terms of the L/C. For a cash contract, the L/C will be issued to allow payment to be made on sight of the documents – a sight L/C. For contracts involving a credit period, the L/C will be issued to allow payment to be made at some future date, e.g. 180 days after shipment or 360 days after sight of documents – a deferred payment L/C.

Referring to Figure 7.6, M Co. (the importer, the buyer, the applicant of the L/C) instructs its bank, Bank M, to open an irrevocable letter of credit in favour of X Co. (the exporter, the seller, the beneficiary of the L/C). The L/C is advised to X Co. through X Co.'s house bank, Bank X. For a cash contract, the sight L/C will set out Bank M's obligation to pay X Co. on presentation of credit-conforming documents though Bank X. The L/C will detail how the payment will be made, e.g. transfer of funds by Bank M on Bank M's receipt of documents, reimbursement by Bank M to Bank X on Bank X's telexed confirmation of their receipt of credit-conforming documents or reimbursement from Bank M's account with a third bank. Bank X's role, as advising, paying or negotiating bank will be defined in the L/C but, unless the letter is confirmed (see below) Bank X will usually only act as a mailbox handling the documentation and passing on the payment to the exporter when they receive funds from the issuing bank.

The use of forfaiting is related to deferred payment L/Cs where there is a period of credit to be financed. Ideally, to discount a deferred payment L/C, the L/C should be issued to allow the exporter to draw bills of exchange on the issuing bank, with the accepted bills of exchange being returned to the exporter against presentation of credit-conforming documents. The forfaiter then discounts the bills of exchange which can be endorsed for payment to the forfaiter. With the issuing bank having accepted the bills of exchange, the L/C falls away and plays no part in the forfaiting transaction. This type of credit is sometimes referred to as an acceptance L/C and is referred to under Article 9aiii of UCP500.

If a deferred payment L/C does not involve bills of exchange, its discount can be more difficult, as the exporter will need to formally assign the rights of payment to the forfaiting company and the advising/paying bank will need to acknowledge that assignment to the forfaiting company. This can complicate the transaction as different forfaiters and banks may have their own wording of assignment documentation. Most banks also make a charge for assignments, and as some banks calculate their assignment fee pro rata to the value of the L/C, the cost can be significant.

With forfaiting, the assignment is normally made after delivery has taken place, documents have been submitted under the L/C and the maturity date has been established. Therefore, the debt purchased by the forfaiter, without recourse to the exporter/beneficiary, is an unconditional and irrevocable payment obligation of the opening bank under the deferred payment L/C.

The forfaiter does not take the documentation risk involved in presentation and negotiation of the documents required under the L/C. The responsibility for submitting credit-conforming documents remains with the exporter as discount only takes place once the documents are accepted, the maturity date is fixed and satisfactory assignment documentation is received by the forfaiter, confirming that payment will be made to the forfaiter at maturity and not to the beneficiary.

As assignments of L/Cs can become involved and complicated they are less attractive to the secondary forfaiting market and therefore the costs of discounting may be higher than if the credit period were evidenced by bills of exchange accepted by the issuing bank under the terms of the L/C.

It is worth mentioning that, partly because of certain countries' legal requirements and restrictions, at the time of writing, at least 50% of all original export transactions financed on an à forfait basis involve L/C. However, since the drawing of bills of exchange under L/Cs was more clearly defined with the introduction of UCP500 in January 1994, the number of transactions involving bills of exchange drawn under L/Cs, rather than L/C assignments has increased significantly.

Finally, we should mention stand by L/Cs. In certain countries, most notably the USA the aval is not recognized as a legal form of guarantee. Buyers in the USA will therefore often offer bank security of payment in the form of a stand by L/C.

The defining characteristic of a stand by L/C is that it only guarantees payment in the event that the buyer (and usually the applicant of the stand by L/C) fails to make payment themselves.

For a stand by L/C to be acceptable to the forfaiter it would normally need to be transferable, to allow the forfaiter to become the beneficiary and it must be issued in a form which allows the forfaiter to make a valid claim for payment in the event that the original obligor (the buyer) fails to make payment to the forfaiter. Obviously, the original debt must also be documented in such a way as to enable the debt to be transferred to and collected by the forfaiter – the most obvious way being the use of bills of exchange or promissory notes. The stand by L/C should ideally allow payment to be made to the forfaiter, after having been transferred, against presentation of a simple statement stating that the original debt had not been paid to the forfaiter at maturity.

In practice the discount of a debt, covered by a stand by L/C, can be quite complicated, involving detailed negotiations between the exporter, the buyer, the issuing bank and the forfaiter to ensure that the debt and stand by L/C can be discounted.

The use of stand by L/Cs is driven by the legal statutes of certain countries, rather than by pragmatic considerations.

Confirmations of letters of credit (full confirmations and silent confirmations)

Under an irrevocable L/C it is the buyer's bank, usually situated in the buyer's country which has given the exporter their promise to pay on presentation of documents. The exporter may not be happy with this level of security, particularly if the buyer's bank is small or is unknown to the exporter or if the buyer's country has had previous payment difficulties, perhaps due to a shortage of hard currency.

For additional security the exporter may insist, under the terms of their supply contract with the buyer, that the L/C is confirmed by a first-class bank in the exporter's country (or some other acceptable third country). Under a confirmed irrevocable L/C, it is the confirming bank (which could again be the issuing bank's correspondent bank or the exporter's house bank) which undertakes to make payment to the exporter on presentation of credit-conforming documents. The exporter still has the responsibility to submit correct documentation under the terms of the L/C and any discrepancies may result in non-payment.

In our example above, assuming that Bank X has confirmed the L/C, Bank X now has a primary payment obligation rather than a mailbox function. Bank X will make a charge for confirming the L/C and whilst it is possible for the confirmation fee to be paid by the buyer, in practice it is almost always the exporter who stands the cost of the confirmation.

The level of the fee will depend on Bank X's perception of the commercial risk (bank default) and political risk (country default) involved. X Co. will, of course, be far more comfortable in having its own house bank's undertaking to pay than it would have been with the undertaking of the overseas issuing bank.

Whether a bank in the exporter's country is willing to give the undertaking, in confirming the credit, will depend on whether they have country and bank limits in place to cover that particular L/C or if they can negotiate some form of cash cover from the issuing bank. Very often, a bank will only add their confirmation to a L/C if the issuing bank requests it to do so. As the issuing bank is aware of the confirmation it is sometimes referred to as a full confirmation.

The comments above regarding the discount of irrevocable deferred payment L/Cs apply equally to confirmed irrevocable deferred payment L/Cs that it is easier and often less expensive to discount a bill of exchange accepted by the confirming bank under the terms of the L/C than it is to discount an assignment of proceeds.

For exports to certain countries, it is often difficult or impossible to obtain a full confirmation of a L/C, as the issuing bank will not request an advising bank to add its confirmation. This may be a matter of policy or a belief that this casts some doubt on the issuing bank's ability to pay. In such cases the advising bank may still be willing to add its confirmation but as this would be unknown to the issuing bank it is often referred to as a silent confirmation.

Some forfaiting companies now undertake significant silent confirmation business. They do this in two ways. First, on the basis of risk participation. If the advising bank is unwilling to confirm the L/C or to take the whole value involved, the forfaiting company may issue their written undertaking to the advising bank to pay in the event that the issuing bank fails to pay against presentation of credit-conforming documents. Second, and more usually, the forfaiting company may issue their written undertaking directly to the exporter/beneficiary. In effect, the forfaiter is giving the advising bank or the exporter their counter-guarantee.

The exporter still has the responsibility to submit credit-conforming documents under the L/C and the forfaiting company will need to be satisfied that the reason for non-payment is not a discrepancy, before they will make payment under the terms of their written undertaking.

Types of market instruments currently used

There is a range of negotiable instruments that can evidence an underlying trade forfait transaction. As stated at the beginning of this section, the most favoured form of negotiable instrument for trading in the forfaiting secondary market is an avalized promissory note. However, the structure used is often a function of regional market practice, tradition and familiarization, rather than the form that is most amenable to the secondary market. Consequently, the typical non-recourse negotiable instruments used in south-east Asia are deferred payment L/Cs with or without accepted bills drawn under the letter of credit. In eastern Europe the typical non-recourse negotiable instruments used will be promissory notes or bills of exchange with an attached aval or separate letter of guarantee or book receivables with a burgschaft (conditional letter of guarantee). In the Americas the typical non-recourse negotiable instruments used will be promissory notes either avalized or sometimes (as in the USA) with an attached stand by L/C.

7.6 Contingent liabilities

It may also be relevant to make a point here regarding *contingent liabilities*. These are liabilities that will only arise to an accounting entity, contingent on the non-performance of another party. An example of this is when an importer's bank avalizes a promissory note. The importer's bank will receive a guarantee fee for this service from the importer but in the importer's bank's balance sheet this potential obligation will only crystallize into an actual liability to the bank, if the importer fails to meet their obligation to the holder of the note at maturity. So the avalizing/guaranteeing bank does not have an actual liability but only a potential liability, which is realized only if the importer fails to meet the note on due date.

Negotiable instruments used to evidence an underlying receivable stream, under most legal systems, are bought and sold with recourse to previous holders and ultimately the exporter, if the negotiable instrument is not met on due date. That is to say in theory all holders will have a contingent liability until the negotiable instrument is met at due date.

Holders of non-recourse negotiable instruments however have forfeited this right of recourse and the instruments are bought and sold without this right, meaning the exporter and each successive holder has no contingent liability. This is the major advantage of forfaiting for the exporters and traders. However, in certain instances there may be a contingent liability even on the exporter of non-recourse instruments if it can be shown that the exporter has not exercised due diligence in the transaction.

What constitutes due diligence? The parameters of this may well be disputed in a legal context at some stage in the future but at present it is an unanswered question. This transaction risk is considered in the next section.

7.7 Transaction, payout and other documentation risks

7.7.1 The transaction risk

A major feature of non-recourse trade credit financing is that the underlying negotiable credit instrument is abstracted from the underlying sales contract. Non-performance on the underlying sales transaction, such as the quality of goods, non-delivery, time, location delays, performance, etc. form the basis of the transaction risk. It is crucial to the forfaiter that the credit finance mechanism is totally abstracted from the payment obligation.

So, although the transaction risk is not *prima facie* a direct risk to the forfaiter it can weigh heavily with the forfaiter. It is certainly not unknown for forfaiters to turn down deals where selling counterparts were not considered good enough for this risk. In order to identify and abstract themselves from this risk, forfaiters may include in their contracts with the exporters a clause(s) as detailed below:

> You warrant that documents submitted to us for discounting under this agreement are enforceable and free title may be and is assigned to us. You warrant that the underlying claim exists. By submitting documents to us you also warrant that the terms of the delivery contract have been correctly fulfilled and that the amount of the claim to be discounted exists. In addition, you confirm to us that you will irrevocably bear any problems relating to the delivery contract, that objections arising from the delivery contract will not be raised against the payment obligations, and that any warranties will be settled directly by you with the customer at your cost.
>
> Any deductions from the discounted claim resulting from any present or future withholding taxes, impost, fees, collection charges or duties or any other taxes of any nature, are for your account.

7.7.2 Payout risks

The exporter. Preparation of forfait documents in continental Europe is often carried out by the exporter's bank, who will send the agreed documentation endorsed to the forfaiter, "without recourse" together with their confirmation that the signatures of the importer, exporter and guarantor, where they appear on the documentation, are authentic and legally and validly binding on the respective companies and banks. Particularly in the UK if the forfaiter has been dealing directly with the exporter, the exporter would usually send the documents directly to the forfaiter. Once the forfaiter declares the forfait documents "clean", i.e. there are no outstanding confirmations or changes required then a value date is agreed and the documents are discounted and the discounted proceeds remitted to the exporter. Usually, although this will depend on what has been previously agreed by the exporter and forfaiter, the net proceeds are paid in accordance with the exporter's instruction to the house bank of the exporter after receipt of clean documentation by the forfaiter. If the documentation is not "clean" the forfaiter may want to enter into an agreement with the exporter whereby they will remit the discounted proceeds under reserve, pending receipt of clean documentation by a certain date. It is this type of flexibility which adds to the appeal of forfait finance. However, as long as a reserve exists the exporter potentially bears the entire transaction risks.

The forfaiter. On receipt of the forfait documentation and before paying out the forfaiter will need confirmations that:

❑ the debt instruments are irrevocable, abstract (independent from the underlying sales contract between the exporter and the importer) and fully and freely transferable
❑ the guarantee is irrevocable, transferable, unconditional and totally abstract from the underlying commercial contract and its performance
❑ there is clear evidence that the debtor/guarantor will pay exclusively in the convertible currency as evidenced on documentation free from any taxes or other deduction whatsoever
❑ all signatures on the documents are confirmed by a bank, or other acceptable entity
❑ the forfaiter reserves the right, even after presentation of documents, to request any additional documentation due perhaps to a change in law or central bank regulations.

At maturity. Usually the forfaiter will have confirmed with the guaranteeing bank some time prior to maturity that they are holding without-recourse negotiable instruments guaranteed by them. This confirmation will detail the amount, currency, issue and maturity date. This is good practice as it can help to pre-empt problems that may otherwise arise at maturity. It is normal form for the holder to present the notes direct to the guarantor bank at maturity, because in this way the guarantor bank can be instructed to pay under its guarantee if the importer cannot pay. The guarantee is an absolute obligation on the guarantor bank and must be met on due date. That is irrespective of any problems between the exporter and the importer, relating to the underlying sales contract. In the event of non-payment of the without-recourse instrument, then the holder only has a legal claim against the importer and the guarantor bank, since any rights against the previous holders or the exporter were foregone. The exception being warranties as stipulated in Section 7.6 (transaction risk).

It should also be noted that if one note in a series is not met this does not amount to an event of default for the holder against the avalizing bank for the remaining notes in the series such that the whole series then is due immediately, which may be the case with a direct loan.

7.7.3 Other documentary risks

Inadequate or unauthorized documentation is a potential risk associated with any paper evidencing or validating an underlying trade or financial obligation. Without-recourse negotiable instruments certainly have no monopoly on this type of risk. However, because the trades are usually across political, economic and legal frontiers, these concerns can often be accentuated by local requirements as regards import licences, the validity of bank guarantees and the remittance of foreign currency. The local regulations are subject to change but it is rare for established documentation that is correct at the time of the transaction to be retrospectively altered by a statutory change in the importing country. The onus therefore lies very much on the forfaiter in the primary market to make sure the documentation is correct, authorized and validated at the time of the exchange of documentation against cash.

Safe custody. Another aspect of the documentary risk is the potential for loss or misappropriation of the negotiable instrument evidencing the underlying debt. This risk should not be underestimated, particularly the potential for physical damage or loss of the instrument. Office procedures, logging systems, recording transactions, division of responsibilities, authorizations and sequential numbering, all need to be set up, adhered to and monitored. Safe custody off- and on-site as applied to any negotiable instrument needs to be implemented. Adequate insurance cover needs to be put in place. However, because of the nature of the instrument with its unique underlying trade transaction, the relatively limited number of counterparties in this market and the standard check procedures, it would be difficult not just for a thief to steal the negotiable instruments but to organize and arrange payment at maturity. This is not impossible, but a without-recourse negotiable instrument is not a standard bearer bond.

Counter-party risk. There is also a counter-party risk which is certainly worth mentioning. This is a risk which is associated with any trade or financial transaction between two parties. Can party A trust party B to undertake and deliver its side of the transaction? This can apply to the relationship between the exporter and the forfaiter in the primary market, or between successive holders of the negotiable instrument in the secondary market.

In each instance the underlying counter-party risk concern must be addressed. Forfaiting counterparties can range from departments of large international banks to individuals working from hotel rooms. The seller of the asset must operate a system such that they receive good value in exchange for the asset. Each forfaiter will have their own set of in-house rules. As the underlying evidence of trade transactions are negotiable instruments both the safe custody and counter-party risk must be addressed by the holder of those instruments.

Bibliography

For further information consider the following:

Alistair Watson, *The Finance of International Trade,* The Institute of Bankers.

William Hedley, *Bills of Exchange and Bankers' Documentary Credits*, Lloyd's of London Press.

Summary

In a few pages it is not possible to do justice to the detail, range, scope and variety of both transport and financial documentation available to meet the payment obligation of trade transactions. However, with regard to forfaiting documentation a few useful pointers can be made.

❑ Documentation evidencing the forfaiting transaction uses one of the instruments outlined in this chapter, or at least some variant.

❑ It is in the interests of all parties to evidence the forfaiting transaction using the most straightforward documentation as regards the payment obligation of a trade transaction. This is a promissory note avalized by an acceptable bank. However, even with convoluted documentation a few simple common-sense checks to and on the parties concerned can establish the *bona fides* of a transaction.

❑ There is a considerable amount of individual country statute and legislation to safeguard the rights of parties to both the trade and the financing of the trade and the instrument used in that trade. These are sometimes potentially in conflict and offer ground for cross-border legal discussion.

❑ There is, however, in reality a general uniformity of statute, even across different legal frontiers. The International Chamber of Commerce Uniform Customs and Practices are a universally recognized set of rules governing the use of documentary credit in international commerce.

❑ Forfait financing is essentially a supplier credit evidenced by a range of payment obligation negotiable instruments, usually guaranteed by a third party. To the point of being both repetitive and tedious, the one characteristic that sets it apart is that it is bought and sold without recourse to previous holders including the exporter, if it is not met at maturity by the importer or guarantor.

EIGHT
How big is the forfaiting market?

8.1	Introduction	8.4	Expansion or contraction?
8.2	The classic forfaiting instrument	8.5	The current picture and summary
8.3	So can we measure this market?		

8.1 Introduction

There have been a number of attempts to quantify the size of the global forfaiting market and none have succeeded. The Bank of England shelved the idea in the mid-1980s, for reasons that centred not so much around the availability of data but rather the problems associated with a credible definition of what a forfaiting trade transaction is. In addition to these definition problems of forfaiting, the non-recourse negotiable instrument is also a free-market instrument and as such there are no publicly available statistical databases.

Various market players, as an alternative to quantifying the actual size of the market, have attempted to quantify the potential size of the forfaiting market at a point in time. In this case one can give full reign to unsubstantiated guesses without having to be too concerned with objective rigour and meaningful definitions.

There is also a further rider in attempting to quantify even the size of the potential market. Are we looking at the primary market paper generated over a certain time period? Or are we quantifying the secondary market? In which case what weighting should we attach to the velocity of circulation of paper in the secondary market?

The absence of a definition and available or even obtainable data means one falls back on platitudes based on subjective value judgement, such as:

> The size of the primary forfaiting market is based on a market familiarity with this free-market export credit instrument and the appropriateness of the instrument to both sellers and buyers for that particular trade and is enhanced by the existence of a secondary market.

This chapter, however, will try to substantiate that at this time the factors for a growth in the primary forfaiting market are stronger than those which would cause a contraction of the market. Since any domestic or international trade could use forfaiting to finance the debt between seller and buyer a case could be made, that the size of the market is limited only by the number of world transactions over a period of time. However, by identifying the circumstances when forfaiting would be the optimum method of finance for trade we may be able to arrive at a more meaningful number.

A further qualification is that using the optimum trade instrument is dependent on circumstances that are by their very nature dynamic.

8.2 The classic forfaiting instrument

The birth and growth of the non-recourse forfaiting market, detailed in Section 1.5, indicates the instrument had at the outset certain characteristics, for example:

- West German *capital exports* (machinery) to Poland.
- *Medium-term* import credit funding up to five years.
- *Ten semi-annual notes* to run from date of shipment.
- Notes *guaranteed* by a bank within the buyer's country.
- *Fixed rate* discounted to net present value.

If this market were not continually changing and adapting and we could possibly estimate values of the forfaited paper being generated in the primary market, even though there are no data published on the transactions in this market, we could obtain the actual capital trade between certain countries and then estimate how much of that uses supplier credit and the proportion that could be attributed to forfaiting.

Even this estimate is increasingly difficult, due to the changing sovereign risk parameters associated with this market and the movement away from forfaiting being used solely to fund the classic forfait trade transaction. We can develop this suggestion by considering the example of what was previously Czechoslovakia.

Slovakia and the Czech Republic

The former Czechoslovakia was an importer of capital goods from western European countries and consequently a source of the classic forfait-paper transaction. A country at that time (1960–70) with a technology gap, short of credit and a fairly limited western bank direct appetite for medium-term Czechoslovakian risk, but with a well-regarded bank administration system and a good history of meeting trade-related payments in full and on due date.

After 1992, following the division of the country, we now find there is a domestic and foreign currency liquidity in the Czech Republic that has resulted in importers often funding imports at more advantageous terms by direct loans from their domestic banks and consequently not using the primary forfait market to the same extent that has historically been the case. Since 1 October 1995 the Czech Crown has been freely convertible. In fact, at the time of writing Czech banks are now actively looking for assets in the secondary forfaiting market which they are keen to put on their balance sheets in exchange for cash.

In Slovakia there are still some classic à forfait transactions but because of a shortage of liquidity, one note six-month forfait paper, often in the form of a deferred payment letter of credit is now being used to fund the import of fuel and commodities. Historically these transactions would have used negotiable instruments with recourse. Why the change? Because there is a developed secondary market that likes the without-recourse characteristic that is the hallmark of forfait paper and this type of funding expands the limited liquidity of the Slovak economy.

Doubtless, at the time of reading this book, the risk parameters of both of these sovereign countries will have a different external perception and utilization of this non-recourse trade and credit instrument than at the time of writing.

8.3 So can we measure this market?

As forfait paper can be evidenced by almost any form of negotiable instrument its sole defining trait is that of non-recourse. No country publishes statistics on without-recourse credit instruments although nearly all countries publish, with a varying range of sophistication, export/import trade statistics. There is no objective credible measure. Although we cannot credibly estimate the size of this market, we can identify the factors that may result in its use by volume and value, expanding or contracting.

However, in spite of all the caveats, it is a bit limp not to try and hang some numbers on the market. In the year ending 31 December 1995 the total turnover of London Forfaiting Company PLC in their audited accounts was approximately $2.0 billion. If the average life of these deals is two-and-three-quarter years and London Forfaiting Company has, say, 25% of the world market. Then this market has a size of $2.0 billion × 2.75 × 4 = $22 billion.

These figures would probably be disputed by players in the forfaiting market, not least London Forfaiting Company. However, what is less in dispute is the approximate split of currencies used in this market. A rough guide at present would be 30% DM, some 55% in US$ and the balance in sterling, Swiss francs, French francs, Swedish krona and yen.

8.4 Expansion or contraction?

Potential growth factors

❏ As finance markets increasingly look to securitize assets forfaiting has a growing importance for trading both short- and medium-term receivables since unlike other trade instruments there is no contingent liability on the seller's books of account.
❏ Free-market economies, a removal of trade restrictions and a reduction in government export credit schemes enhance the use of this type of instrument.
❏ An increasing awareness of the existence of forfaiting and its applicability in certain circumstances combined with the fashion for emergent market risks on a variety of secondary market instruments, some far more exotic than non-recourse trade-related negotiable instruments.
❏ Its flexibility, which may create definition problems but enhances its amoeba-like growth in both the trade and finance markets.
❏ The maturity of the secondary market after 40 years of banks and finance houses trading a forfaited paper in part gives the primary market a certain vitality.

- ❏ Its potential to evidence financial obligations in addition to trade finance receivables.
- ❏ Its ability to be attached to existing negotiable trade and financial instruments within existing sovereign legislation.
- ❏ At this point national export credit agencies appear to be contracting state support to their exporters and relying increasingly on the free market. At the same time it appears to be the case that the creditworthy world is expanding.

Potential limiting factors

- ❏ Restrictions on cross-border trade and an increasing isolationism by some sovereign economies.
- ❏ A secondary market which has no depth or liquidity.
- ❏ Sovereign statute that restricts the non-recourse aspect of negotiable instruments.
- ❏ Sovereign statute that restricts the transfer of negotiable instruments.
- ❏ A major fraud or dislocation in the market.

8.5 The current picture and summary

The forfaiting market is a minute market in the context of world trade. However, in the context of a specialist central European trading instrument it has grown and matured over the last 40 years to be and acknowledged as being a free-trade export credit finance instrument that can be of great value to exporters, importers, banks and finance houses in certain circumstances. For the market to develop it requires specialized forfaiters and forfaiting departments in clearing banks to generate primary paper from their customer base, savings banks that will hold or trade that paper, specialist trading houses that will trade the market and turnover their forfaiting assets as much as six times a year and merchant banks that will advise the professional market makers. At this point in time the growth factors would appear to be in the ascendancy. Whatever the current size of either the primary or secondary market, if the experience of the last 40 years is anything to go by, next year the forfaiting market will continue its assumed but as yet unquantified year-on-year growth.

NINE

Accounting issues, profit and portfolio valuation

9.1 Introduction
9.2 Book-keeping
9.3 Rules of accounting
9.4 Accounts and time periods
9.5 The valuation of closing stock
9.6 An example. The Forfaiting Company
9.7 Marking the asset to market value
9.8 Three optional accounting strategies

9.1 Introduction

Statutory accounts which categorize historical data are usually based on double-entry book-keeping, which is conventionally attributed to the founding father of accounting, Lucca Pacioli, a Benedictine monk who in 1494 wrote what was basically a mathematics textbook: *Summa de Arithmetica Geometria, Proportioni et Proportionalita*.

At that time in Renaissance Italy large tracts of land and its associated produce were owned by powerful families who would appoint agents to run their estates and the agents would periodically report back to the families as to how the underlying trades were progressing or had progressed. Amongst the families' concerns, the most basic was: is the agent stealing from me?

9.2 Book-keeping

Pacioli didn't discover accounting as such, since single-entry and variants of double-entry had undoubtedly existed since trade had started. However, he did codify the accrual system of recording transactions. Starting with an opening balance sheet at a point in time, and opening the ledgers (1) appropriate to the accounting entity at that time and then recording the transactions over a period of time and entering them in the ledgers. At the end of a period of time or more likely, in Pacioli's day, the completion of a trade, the ledgers would be closed off (2). A trial balance consisting of all the net balances would be drawn up as a memo account (3). Then certain adjustments would be made to the ledgers (4) to take into account the actual expenses of the period and the amount of assets used up or reduced in value during the trading period. The revenue and expense ledgers would then be closed off to the profit and loss account (5). The residual profit or loss being accredited to the owners and all the remaining open ledgers would then be brought down to give the closing balance sheet at a point in time (6).

Early time   Later time

(1) open ledger accounts

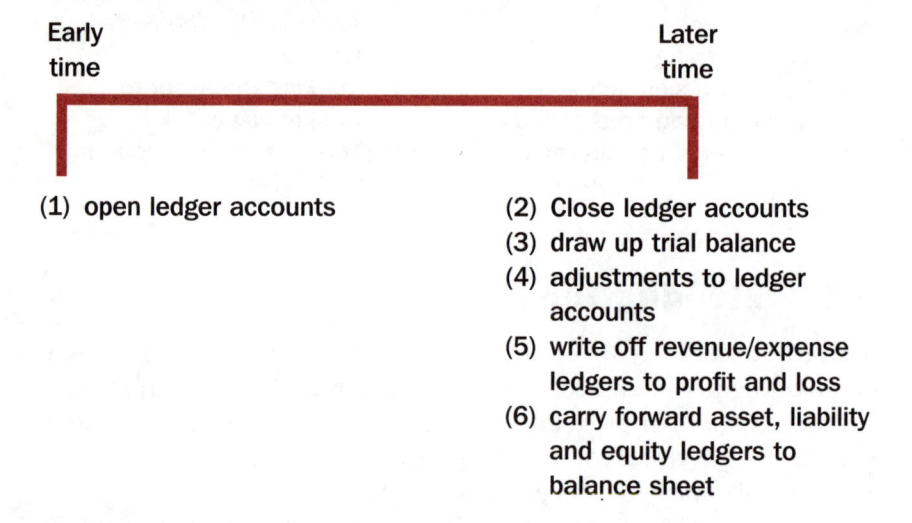

(2) Close ledger accounts
(3) draw up trial balance
(4) adjustments to ledger accounts
(5) write off revenue/expense ledgers to profit and loss
(6) carry forward asset, liability and equity ledgers to balance sheet

Figure 9.1 Keeping a set of accounts over a trading period.

Did this double-entry accruals method of recording data, giving a profit and loss account over time and a balance sheet at a point in time, stop agents from stealing from the families they worked for? Probably not, particularly if the agent's intention was a one-off theft. However, it did make it far harder for any agent intent on misappropriation to keep up the falsification of accounts over periods of time or successive trades without becoming snared in a tangled web of false numbers.

The statutory and accounting bodies in various free-market economies would claim, and rightly so, that although there are differences between how the agents in Pacioli's time and the directors of today's accounting entities record their trading transactions to report back to their owners or shareholders. They would however probably also agree that the method used today is fundamentally the same as that used 500 years ago and more importantly for the purposes of this chapter the rules of accounting (both statutory and management) have also not altered.

9.3 Rules of accounting

- conservative/prudent
- consistency
- objectivity
- entity.

9.3.1 Conservative/prudent

"Always look on the bright side of life", may be or may have been a popular song, but one thing is for certain, it was not sung by an accountant. An accountant in books of account will always imagine the worst. If there is a bluebird out there then an accountant is obliged to ignore it, on the other hand if, metaphorically, it looks like rain an accountant will assume it will rain. Why? Because an accountant is prudent. They may have wildly exciting social lives, but professionally they are prudent and are trained financially to imagine the worst. Consequently an accountant will value a current asset at the lower of cost or market value.

Time	No. of shares	Price per share	Market cost or book value
Early time	1000	£10	£10,000
Later time (A)	1000	now £20	?
Later time (B)	1000	now £5	?

Figure 9.2

At later time (A) if the price of the share has risen to £20, the accountant will put the total book value in his or her accounts at £10,000. The point needs to be made that if the accountant had sold the shares he or she would receive gross proceeds of £20,000. But until such a time as the sale is actually made the total book value is

£10,000. Why? Because the accountant is prudent and will not take into account a profit until that profit has actually been realized. The accountant will value the shares at the lower of cost or market value and not at their anticipated current market price.

Similarly the corollary also holds. So at later time (B) if the price of the share has fallen to £5 per share, the accountant will put the total book value in the accounts at £5000. The accountant will take into account a loss as soon as that loss is anticipated. The accountant will value the shares at the lower of cost or market value. Why? Because one of the fundamental rules of accountancy is to be prudent.

Assets are *not* valued in the books of account at their current street value but according to certain accounting rules, one of which is prudence. It may just be that the book value and the street value are one and the same but that would be, probably to the dismay of various accounting bodies around the world, merely coincidence.

9.3.2 Consistency

Another rule of the accounting game is that accountants will always be consistent. Even if they are wrong, at least there is the benefit of being consistently wrong. This may sound like a rather questionable benefit. However, perhaps I can illustrate this benefit with an example. Faced with a choice of red or black, an individual consistently chooses black although red is the correct choice. Provided the individual is consistent then a third party can always choose the opposite to the individual and as a consequence will always be right, provided the individual is consistent. The important feature therefore is not the choice of the individual, but is that if the individual changes his or her choice *a priori* he or she should let third parties know so that they can take appropriate action in this new set of circumstances.

In most countries either by statute, accounting recommendation or convention there will be a section on accounting policies in the notes to the accounts, the first note or a preface to the first note to the accounts. These policies will identify how the entity deals with depreciation of assets, research and development expenditure, advertising expenditure, valuation of closing stock, revaluation of fixed assets and other accounting issues that will impact the residual profit (loss) before tax figure, for the relevant trading period. It may be the case that a change in profit is due not to a change in trading performance but to a change in accounting policy. However, this information even *post hoc* (and statutory accounts are axiomatically *post hoc*), will be of considerable value provided that any changes are detailed in the accounting policies section of the notes to the account.

9.3.3 Objectivity

Accountants love headed notepaper sent to an accounting entity by a third party. Invoices from suppliers, bank statements, valuations at a point in time from a respected body or a well-traded market – all these imply arm's length, independent, objective, corroboration. This is meat and drink to an accountant and particularly to an auditor. If the directors of an accounting entity suggest a valuation of a traded asset, however informed that valuation, it is perceived and consequently downgraded as being their, albeit informed, subjective value judgement of an asset in an entity in which they have a vested interest.

9.3.4 Entity

The final rule of accounting procedures in this particular classification is perhaps the one that we should have started with and it is quite simply that of the accounting/legal entity to which the accounts relate. Accounting entities can be sole traders, partnerships or a variety of corporate bodies or companies. Terms such as debtors and creditors only become meaningful when they relate to the accounts of a particular accounting entity. It is readily apparent, but bears restating, that the sales on credit of a particular entity which are shown as debtors in that entity's books of account are shown in the customer's books of account as creditors. The question of what entity are we buying from, selling to, borrowing from, lending to, working for and so on only has meaning when the entity itself is identified.

As a rider to the question: "To which entity do these accounts relate?" should be added the question: "Why am I looking at these accounts?". Is it because you are a potential shareholder, or a supplier looking to assess whether the company can pay you, or an employee, or the tax collector, VAT collector, a debtor concerned about after care or an existing shareholder, or a trader looking to purchase a receivable stream evidenced by a negotiable instrument? Each will have a different perspective, a range of interests and concerns in looking at the accounts of that particular entity.

9.4 Accounts and time periods

There are other rules of the accounting game; materiality, going-concern basis, but I would focus for our purposes of assessing profit and portfolio valuation on prudence, consistency, subjectivity and entity.

There is, of course, one further major factor we should consider: time. Any profit and loss statement is over a period of time. Usually for statutory accounts this will be for a 12-month period. Of course, this is only a relatively recent tradition, but it is now the internationally accepted norm. However, the profit and loss account can relate to any time period. We have seen under the accruals system of accounting that the expenses for a period, irrespective of whether they have been paid or even invoiced, will be accrued into the relevant accounting period. However, the revenue stream can be more difficult to assess, particularly when it is generated over a period greater than the profit and loss period. Consequently, the profit on a transaction can become, in part, a function of the allocation of unrealized revenue over a series of profit and loss time periods, subject to the accounting rules.

For example, let us take a fixed discount rate promissory note payable in three years' time. There will be a running yield (discount rate less cost of funding rate) and also at each point in time a market valuation based on the discounted cash flow to net present value (NPV). The accounting issues according to the rules of the game are already beginning to loom, however before we look at an actual example let us highlight one final concern – the valuation of closing stock.

9.5 The valuation of closing stock

The valuation of closing stock becomes an essential figure in the profit calculation of any company which carries material stock levels relative to its sales revenue figure. In Figure 9.3 if the closing stock is valued not at 32, but increased to say 52. Then by following through the example the resultant cost of goods sold will be 3, the gross profit 57, the expenses remain at 10, so the net profit figure will be 57 as opposed to 37. Increasing the closing stock value inflates profits and increases the stock valuation in the balance sheet. The following year the entity will have to pay the price of inflated stock values.

	£	£
Sales revenue (price × volume)		60
Opening stock	0	
Purchases	55	
	55	
Less closing stock	32	
Cost of goods sold		23
Gross profit		37
Expenses		10
Net profit		27

Figure 9.3 The profit and loss account for the period (figures are illustrative, this is the first year of operation of this manufacturing company).

Of course the first three rules of accounting prevent the closing stock valuation and consequently the profit figure from being an arbitrary number.

❏ Prudence means that accountants will value stock at the lower of cost or market value, so the profit will tend to be understated.
❏ Consistency means the same method of stock valuation will continue to be used over successive trading periods so different stock valuation methods will even themselves out over time. To change the stock valuation method would only allocate profit into different time periods.
❏ Objectivity means that there must be some form of third party corroboration of the stock valuation.

As an aside, most creative accounting opportunities (putting the residual profit or loss figure where you want it) that are within the rules of accounting hinge around the decision, when an expenditure is made, it is to acquire an asset, or is it an expense?

Our focus is now not on a company buying and selling or manufacturing goods but on a company buying and selling financial assets. This could be a clearing, merchant or trading bank or more specifically for our purposes a company buying and selling forfaiting assets. Let us take it as a given that this company will acquire only one promissory note (details are given below). This should give us an opportunity to raise the two core accounting issues of forfaiting assets:

1 **Revenue allocation over time.**
2 **The valuation of closing stock.**

That is of course while still playing to the rules of accounting.

9.6 An example. The Forfaiting Company

The Forfaiting Company (TFC) acquired one without-recourse promissory note on 1 January 1995. The promissory note related to a shipment of mining equipment from a Newcastle engineering company with a face value of DM10,000,000 payable by the Indonesian importer in three years' time. The note was avalized by a prime Indonesian bank.

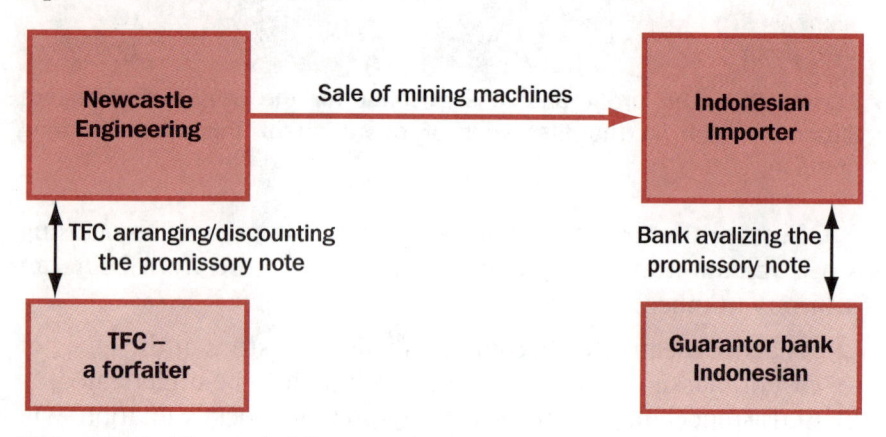

Figure 9.4 The underlying promissory note transaction.

The promissory note was discounted annually at a discount rate of 10%. So in exchange for the note and documentation TFC paid DM7,513,000 to the Newcastle engineering company.

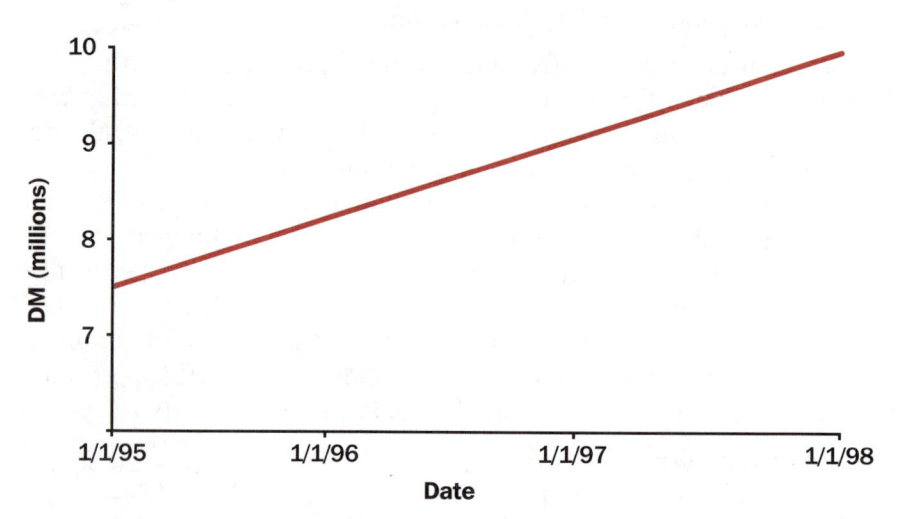

Figure 9.5 The underlying trade credit value.

Accounting issues

TFC have an asset discounted at an interest rate of 10% (the three-year DM interbank interest rate is, say, 6% and the current perceived credit risk margin on the three-year risk on the Indonesian bank guaranteeing the risk is 4%).

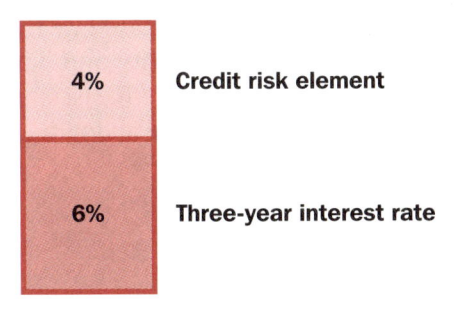

Figure 9.6 The discount rate at 10%.

So the present value of DM10,000,000 at an annual discount rate of 10% on 1 January 1995 is

$$A = P/(1+ \text{discount rate})^t$$
$$A = 10,000,000/(1.10)(1.10)(1.10)$$
$$A = 10,000,000/(1.31)$$
$$A = 7,513,000$$

TFC can hold or trade the instrument.

If TFC decide to trade the instrument on 1 January 1995 then the accounting treatment is straightforward and a net profit or loss will be made on the transaction depending on the discount rate agreed between TFC and the purchasing counter-party. This trade will fulfil all the accounting requirements of prudence, objectivity, entity and consistency. Also, as after the sale TFC has no promissory note, there is no stock valuation to consider and due to the non-recourse nature of forfaiting there is no contingent liability on TFC's books. When both sides of the buy and sell fall within the trading period there are no subjective accounting concerns.

However this is not the case if TFC decide to hold the promissory note across a trading period.

We know that value at a point in time is a function of the discount rate, which in turn comprises the cost of funding and the perceived credit risk (Figure 9.6). With many financial instruments market value can be objectively quantified, as there is likely to be a screen-driven objective price that can at least be used as a basis for current value. So for many financial instruments marking its value to market across a trading period can be objectively substantiated.

Fixed rate non-recourse negotiable trade instruments, usually bank guaranteed by the importer's bank, generated by the unique underlying trade transaction, payable at maturity and held over a trading period, considerably broaden the subjective scope for a range of accounting approaches. We can break these down into five areas for consideration.

9.7 Marking the asset to market value

❏ Case one: revenue allocation with matched funding
❏ Case two: revenue allocation with unmatched funding
❏ Case three: matching funding then trading the asset
❏ Case four: marking the asset to market
❏ Case five: asset/liability currency mismatch.

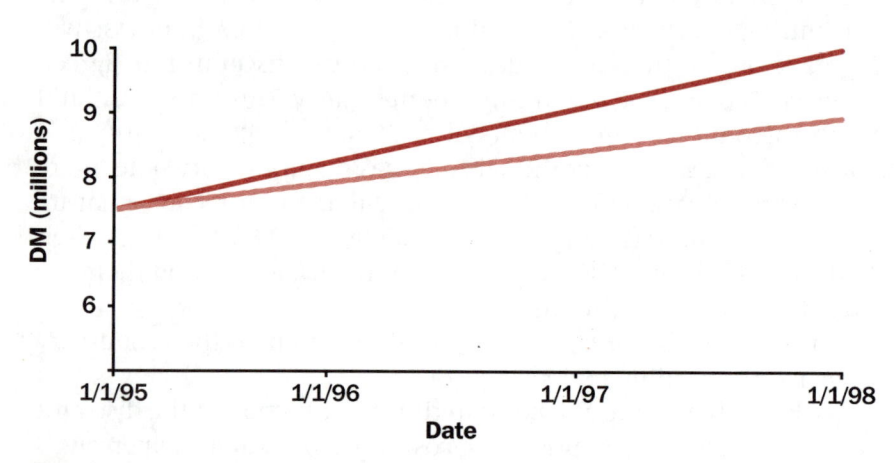

Figure 9.7 Funding considerations and profitability.

9.7.1 Case one

Assuming TFC can obtain three-year funding at an interest rate of 6% and does so; and the credit risk remains a constant throughout the life of the promissory note. Then the lower line in Figure 9.7 represents the cash required at 1 January 1995 to buy the note and annual compound interest rate $[P = A(1+.06)^t]$ to fund the purchase and carry the cost of the underlying asset. As at 1 January 1998 the cash required to purchase the note + compound interest $(P) = 7,513,000 \times (1.06)(1.06)(1.06)$; so $P = $ DM8,948,103.

An accounting question arising in this case is, as at year ending 1 January 1996 do we take the profit as one-third of the eventual anticipated profit $(10,000,000 - 8,948,103 = 1,051,897/3 = 350,632)$? Or do we take no profit until the profit is realized on 1 January 1998? Or do we use another method of anticipated profit allocation? Any method can be used provided it is prudent, consistent and objective and the auditors have no objections.

9.7.2 Case two

Perhaps TFC cannot get hold of three-year funding and can, say, only find one-year funds on the DM interbank rate at, say, 5%. TFC decides to buy an interest swap/option to hedge out the remaining two-year fixed rate risk on the underlying instrument.

Following on from case one there is again the same element of choice as to where you put the profit figure. Also how do you net out the cost of the two-year hedge from 1 January 1996 to 1 January 1998. Is it allocated over this two-year period? Or set-off against the increased net profit in the first year, due to the proportionately cheaper cost of one year funds? Again any method can be used provided it is prudent, consistent and objective and the auditors have no objections.

9.7.3 Case three

If the intention is to sell the asset before its maturity date but funds have been acquired for the asset's lifetime or a derivative is acquired to offset the potential interest rate risk and if the asset is then sold; then TFC has surplus funds it has to put back into the market, or needs to acquire another similarly yielding asset. The accounting treatment for each of these positions over the end of the accounting period again allows great scope for shuffling profits between accounting periods. Again any method can be used provided it is prudent, consistent and objective and the auditors have no objections.

9.7.4 Case four

The time value of money and the consequent cost of funds over different time periods are likely to vary over the lifetime of the promissory note. If the asset is funded short and if the consequent interest rate risk is not hedged this will result in windfall revenue profits or losses. These potential losses should not be underestimated.

However, it is the credit risk, with its related margins which can result in a capital loss or capital gain and is usually perceived as the more likely factor that may cause a rapid erosion of the capital base of a company. The loading in the discount rate for the credit risk in our example is 4%. If the Indonesian bank fails then the credit risk becomes 100% with no recourse against previous holders of the promissory note by the holder of the note at maturity. It is the case that in an imperfect market the perceived credit risk margin is a major factor in creating the range of the bid offer spread through its impact on the discount rate used to calculate the present value of a promissory note. .

At the end of the accounting period, the value of the promissory note is a subjective value judgement and within the constraints only of prudence and consistency, profit can be allocated to different trading periods. The value will depend on the view taken on the credit risk of the guarantor of the promissory note and the consequent element in the discount rate factor allocated to the credit risk. The valuation of the promissory note as at the end of the accounting period is a crunch number and will have a major impact on the trading result allocated to that period.

9.7.5 Case five

Briefly, a further consideration is whether the underlying asset is in the same currency as the funding for that asset. If it isn't then there will be an exchange rate risk and the potential for windfall profits or losses with an associated variety of accounting methods to allocate those windfall gains or losses. If TFC wishes to punt the exchange rate risk market there are far better and more efficient ways of doing it than using a promissory note as the underlying asset. However, even if the asset and its associated funding are in the same currency, there will still be an exchange rate risk until the cash losses or gains are transferred and held in the reporting currency.

9.8 Three optional accounting strategies

Using the same example, let us consider three accounting strategies for TFC as at 1 January 1996 after the company has held the asset for one year as shown in Figure 9.8.

Given:

1 TFC acquired a promissory note on 1 January 1995 with a maturity value on 1 January 1998 of DM10,000,000 for a purchase price of DM7,513,000.
2 TFC obtained three-year funding of DM7,513,000 at an annual interest rate of 6%, payable annually.

9.8.1 First accounting strategy as at 1 January 1996

In this first example, assuming no other revenue, taxation, expenses, other assets or liabilities. TFC has not allocated any revenue on the transaction but has taken into account the interest expense due. The asset is valued at cost.

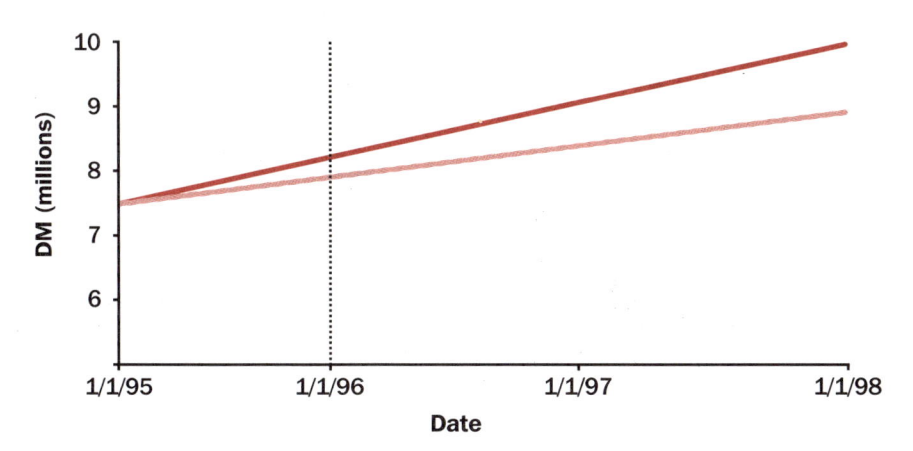

Figure 9.8 Three accounting strategies for TFC as at 1 January 1996.

	Balance sheet as at 1/1/96	Profit and loss Year ending 1/1/96
	Assets = liabilities + equity +	(revenue − expenses)
Promissory note	7,513,000 = 7,513,000	
Interest	450,780	−450,780
Revenue		0
Total	7,513,000 = 7,963,780 +	(450,780)

In this example TFC has made a loss in the trading year of DM450,780. TFC is insolvent, the negative equity being equal to the amount of the loss.

9.8.2 Second accounting strategy as at 1 January 1996

In this second example, again assuming no other revenue, taxation, expenses, other assets or liabilities, TFC has allocated one-third of the net revenue (10,000,000 − 7,513,000 = 2,487,000/3 = 829,000) on the transaction and has taken into account the interest expense due. The asset is now valued at cost plus allocated revenue.

	Balance sheet as at 1/1/96	Profit and loss Year ending 1/1/96
	Assets = liabilities + equity +	(revenue − expenses)
Promissory note	7,513,000 = 7,513,000	
Interest	450,780	−450,780
Revenue	829,000	829,000
Total	8,342,000 = 7,963,780 +	378,220

In this example, the only variable being the accounting treatment, TFC has made a profit in the trading year of DM378,220. TFC is solvent, the equity being equal to the amount of the net profit. The asset is valued at cost plus allocated revenue. Also as the revenue is a subjective judgement it is relatively easy, within the rules of accountancy of consistency and prudence, to attach a range of values to the revenue stream. However, it must be emphasized that all TFC is doing is putting profit into different accounting periods, it is not creating profit.

9.8.3 Third accounting strategy as at 1 January 1996

In this third example, again assuming no other revenue, taxation, expenses, other assets or liabilities, TFC has allocated a one-third of the net revenue (10,000,000 − 7,513,000 = 2,487,000/3 = 829,000) on the transaction and has taken into account the interest expense due. However, due to re-rating of the Indonesian bank risk from 4% to 1%, the relevant discount rate is now 7%. The asset is now valued at face value less two years' annual discount of 7%. Value = 10,000,000/((1.07)(1.07)) = 8,734,387. This gives a capital gain of 8,734,387 − 8,342,000 = 392,387.

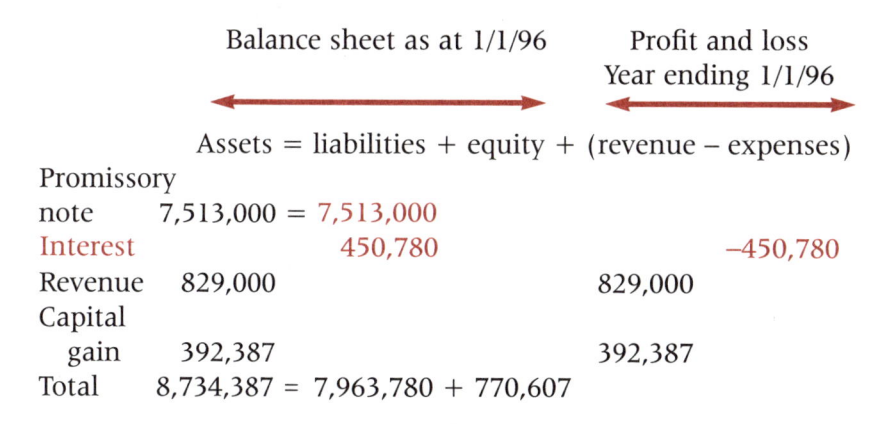

Balance sheet as at 1/1/96 Profit and loss Year ending 1/1/96

Assets = liabilities + equity + (revenue − expenses)

Promissory note	7,513,000 = 7,513,000	
Interest	450,780	−450,780
Revenue	829,000	829,000
Capital gain	392,387	392,387
Total	8,734,387 = 7,963,780 + 770,607	

In this example, bearing in mind the only variable is the accounting treatment, TFC has now made a net profit in the trading year of DM770,607. TFC is solvent, the equity being equal to the amount of the net profit. The asset is valued at market cost.

In this third example, however, the accounting rule of prudence has been well and truly crossed. As assets are valued at the lower of cost or market value. Only if the asset is sold on 1 January 1996 would the above treatment be acceptable to TFC's auditors.

However, if there is a re-rating downwards of the credit risk, not only is it prudent from an accounting viewpoint, it is, if TFC wishes to trade over time, a smart move to regularly mark its assets to the lower of cost or market value.

Summary

❏ Irrespective of whether it is from the perspective of the exporter, the holder or the guarantor, each entity will have an accounting opportunity to allocate profits over different time periods as the tenor of a promissory note can often stretch over a number of accounting periods. This accounting "opportunity" can be further accentuated by the accounting treatment of any associated hedging instruments.

❏ Also, because each instrument is generated by a unique underlying trade deal, the valuation of each instrument at a point can be subject to a wider spread than say a screen-based financial instrument traded in a perfect market.

❏ It is therefore in the interest of all parties that the accounting rules of prudence, consistency, entity and as far as possible objectivity need to be closely adhered to by any entity involved in this non-recourse negotiable trade finance instrument.

TEN

Exporter's "how to" guide

	Introduction	10.3	Option
10.1	Initial sales inquiry from	10.4	Contracts signed
	Gdansk	10.5	Firm bid and commitment
10.2	First indication from	10.6	Shipment and
	forfaiter		documentation

Introduction

Forfaiting is flexible and can, in theory, be used on any occasion or whenever there is value to be received. However, it is usually, and has historically been, associated with medium-term cross-border funding of capital goods. In this section I am going to detail the sequence of events of a *"plain vanilla"* forfaiting transaction involving an engineering company in Liverpool exporting machinery parts to a tractor manufacturing plant in Gdansk.

Sequence of events:

❏ step 1: initial sales inquiry from Gdansk

❏ step 2: first indication from forfaiter

❏ step 3: option

❏ step 4: contracts signed

❏ step 5: firm bid and commitment

❏ step 6: shipment and documentation.

110 Forfaiting for exporters

10.1 Initial sales inquiry from Gdansk

The Liverpool company ascertains that the Gdansk company wishes to buy approximately DM10 million of tractor manufacturing machinery parts, inclusive of any loan interest due. There is considerable competition for this valuable sales contract.

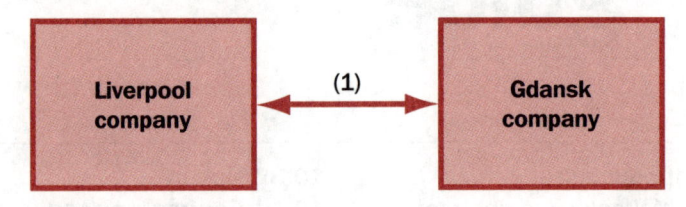

Figure 10.1 Step 1.

The Liverpool company sends out a sales team to Gdansk to discuss the client's exact needs and how they can secure the order. It is readily apparent that the Gdansk company is unwilling to use current scarce cash resources or drawdown existing domestic direct bank loan facilities to pay for the machinery parts. However, the Gdansk company is fairly certain that it should generate enough DM from the sales of the tractors to pay future cash obligations out of future cashflow generated by the anticipated tractor sales. The Gdansk company, who are delighted by the quality of the Liverpool company's product, say to secure the order the supplying company will also have to arrange the finance for the purchase of tractor manufacturing machinery parts.

10.2 First indication from forfaiter

The Liverpool company considers whether it is willing to defer payment by giving credit for a three- to five-year period to the Gdansk company. Balance sheet constraints mean that they decide against this course of action. It needs to find a third party to take over its risk. It contacts its bank, an insurance company, the Export Credit Guarantee Department (ECGD) and a forfaiter to find out whether they can arrange finance for its potential Gdansk client and if so on what terms.

There is a range of methods of finance and credit. However, a combination of the unknown credit standing of the client, the period of credit required and the Polish sovereign risk, limit the buyer's financing opportunities. The Liverpool company should investigate

Exporter's "how to" guide 111

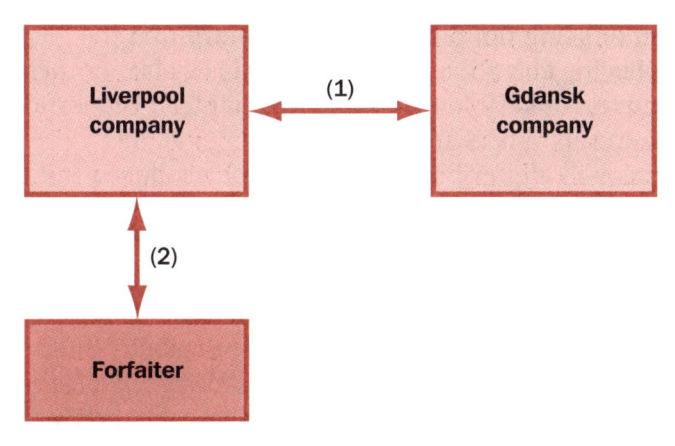

Figure 10.2 Step 2.

all opportunities in order to help it make the sale. The method chosen must be the one that is appropriate in the unique set of circumstances to this particular transaction. Briefly, the bank is likely to suggest some sort of trade finance instrument, perhaps using forfaiting or ECGD, which is a state-backed system for assisting exporters. ECGD has been of invaluable assistance to exporters but is sometimes perceived as being restrictive, bureaucratic and inflexible. Insurance companies are also sometimes willing to consider sovereign and corporate risk for a fee. However, forfaiting is the most likely financial credit to be used, and in this instance non-recourse paper could be the most appropriate.

The Liverpool company will need to contact the forfaiting section of the trade department of a bank or a specialist forfaiter. At this stage the forfaiter will need to know the following:

- what is being sold
- the name and country of the importer and of the guarantor
- the currency, amount and repayment schedule sought
- estimated shipment date
- perhaps an indication of the interest rate the importer is prepared to pay as part of the exporter's supplier credit.

The forfaiter having been given the indicative information will decide whether they can assist the Liverpool company and on what terms and conditions. Most banks or specialist forfaiters enjoy their reputation of being not only flexible but almost on the basis of one phone call being able to say whether a deal is viable for them or not, or how a deal could become workable. Chapter 11 looks at specific examples on this very issue.

Forfaiters will all have different risk profiles, but in this instance let's assume the forfaiter wants to be involved. They can calculate the net payout value the Liverpool company will receive once they have shipped the goods according to the terms of the sales contract and once they have received good documentation. One reason why forfaiting is being increasingly used is this flexibility and the speed of response to the exporter.

In our example, at this point all parties know that machinery parts are being sold and the name and country of the importer. The parties to the transaction may not know at this stage the name of the guarantor bank in the importer's country but provided it is a bank that is acceptable to the forfaiter, this will not present a problem.

All parties know the currency of the trade and the invoice amount (capital and interest) is approximately DM10 million. The forfaiter can detail a repayment schedule with the exporter. Let's say this takes the form of a series of ten promissory notes, each of DM1,000,000 payable semi-annually from the shipment date. Using this information the forfaiter can give the exporter an indication of the cash payout figure they would receive following shipment and exchange of documentation. This may give the Liverpool company some scope for manoeuvre in the sales invoice contract price. The Liverpool company can also indicate to the Gdansk company the banks that it would like to have guarantee the negotiable instruments evidencing the Liverpool company's receivables.

The credit standing of the Polish guaranteeing bank is the main factor in setting the credit margin over the cost of funds and the discount rate to be used by the forfaiter. There is at this important stage continual dialogue between the exporter and the forfaiter. To date no charges have been made or are due, but it must be understood that there is no commitment in place from the forfaiter to purchase this transaction. However, the exporting company may wish to take up an option on the terms and conditions offered by the forfaiter.

10.3 Option

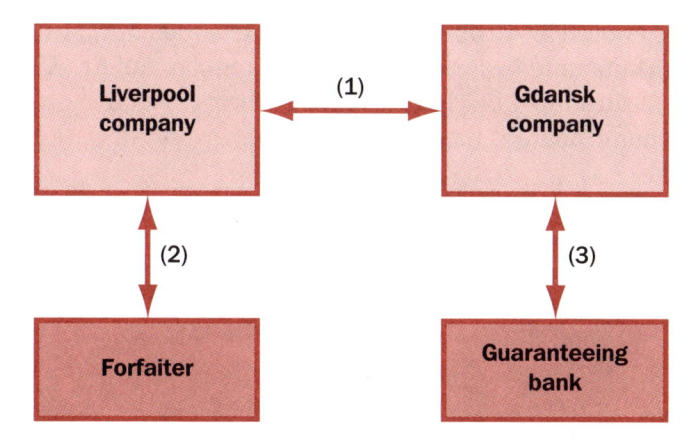

Figure 10.3 Step 3.

At this stage the Gdansk company will enter discussions with the bank that will guarantee the company's trade paper. In this example the bank is likely to be Polish and the Gdansk company's usual banker. The bank will charge an annual fee for this, the terms will vary depending on the guaranteeing banks appetite for the credit and the structure and pricing of the bank's contingent liabilities. The Gdansk company will arrange this directly with the bank.

If the Liverpool Company wishes to fix the terms and conditions offered by the forfaiter they will take up what is referred to as an option with the forfaiter on those terms and conditions. Subject to the underlying sales contract being signed and satisfactory documentation the forfaiter will agree to stand by the terms and conditions agreed between the two parties.

The forfaiter will charge an option fee to run from the date of the option to the date of the conclusion of the successful signing of the export contract, or to the termination of the option because the underlying sales contract has been frustrated. The fee is usually invoiced separately and payable in advance.

The point must be made that a *financial option* usually gives the buyer of that *option* a right and not an obligation, In the case of forfaiting transactions this is definitely not the case, an option in forfaiting parlance means there is an obligation on both parties to stand by the agreed terms and conditions, provided that, for example, the underlying sales contract is signed.

It is unlikely, but the option may also be subject to the forfaiter seeing various authorized and authorizing documents specific to that transaction. This is not as tortuous as it sounds but it does mean that the forfaiter and exporter need to be in regular and timely contact and both parties must be clearly aware of their respective obligations to each other. However, the exporter may not want an option.

10.4 Contracts signed

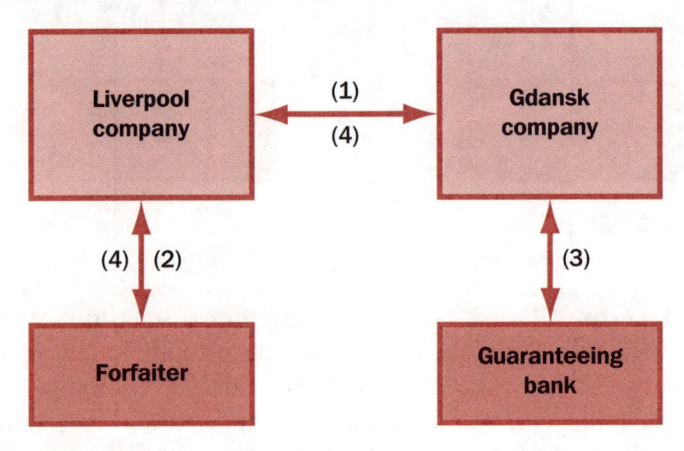

Figure 10.4 Step 4.

The Liverpool company and the Gdansk company sign a sales contract which details the legal obligations on both parties. The Liverpool company must exercise its option with the forfaiting company, the forfaiting contract is signed and now both the forfaiter and the exporter are committed to the terms and conditions of the forfaiting contract.

The terms of the forfaiting agreement will abstract the forfaiting company from any legal obligations if the underlying sales contract for whatever reason is not successfully concluded. In order to expedite the trade the forfaiter does have a responsibility, albeit only a moral obligation to use its experience in such matters as special licences or to inform if particular conditions or authorizations apply or are required by either party.

Again one must stress that forfaiting is flexible. For example, during a period of interest rate volatility or credit uncertainty the forfaiter may limit the option either by period or subject to certain events taking place or not taking place.

10.5 Firm bid and commitment

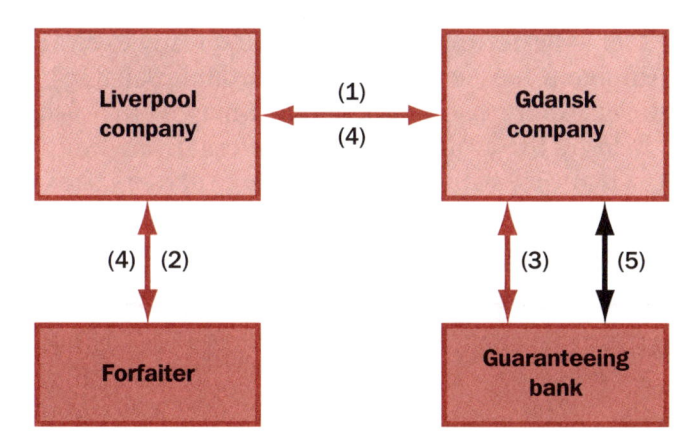

Figure 10.5 Step 5.

If the Liverpool company had decided against taking an option it would ask the forfaiter for a firm bid immediately prior to the sales contract signing or possibly even after the sales contract signing. A firm bid may be described as a committing offer to purchase the suggested transaction without recourse to the exporter valid for acceptance by the exporter usually for one or a maximum of two working days. By nature these firm offers are made free of charge to the exporter but subject to satisfactory documentation to the forfaiter. It has to be understood that firm offers are only requested if and when the exporter has the serious intention to enter into the forfaiting agreement based on the signed delivery contract. Whether the terms and conditions of the forfaiting contract between the Liverpool company and the forfaiter are based on a firm bid at or around the sales contract signing date between the exporter and the importer or based on the agreed option with the forfaiter, both parties are now committed to the terms and conditions of the forfaiting contract.

The Gdansk company could now arrange for the negotiable documentation to be prepared. In our example the transaction is to be evidenced by ten avalized promissory notes. The Gdansk company would probably use its own house bank to prepare the promissory notes, although it is often the forfaiter or exporter who may provide the blank promissory notes.

The Gdansk Company would then get the avalizing bank (guaranteeing bank) to put its aval on the series of promissory notes. These notes have yet to be dated but are in place and ready to be discounted once the shipment has been made. They would probably be held in trust by the exporter's bank, sometimes it may be the case that the notes are held by the avalizing bank or alternatively until after the shipment, when they would be sent to the exporter's bank.

10.6 Shipment and documentation

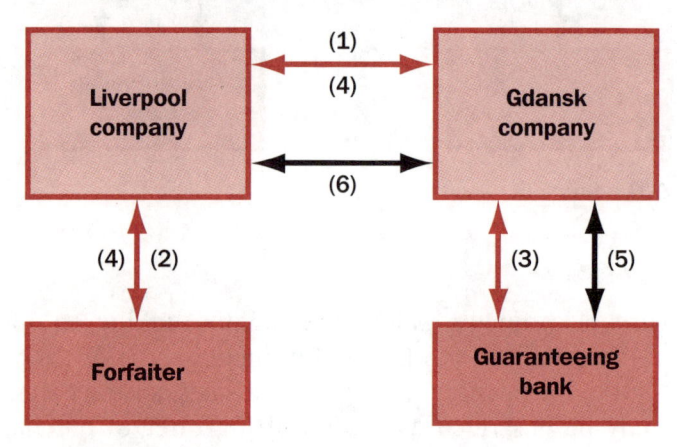

Figure 10.6 Step 6.

Following the shipment (step 6) by the Liverpool company of machinery parts to the Gdansk company, the Liverpool company will take the shipping documents to their bank if that is where the promissory notes are being held and the relevant issue date and maturity date will be written on the promissory notes.

Having added the issue and maturity dates, these promissory notes would be sent to the Liverpool company. The Liverpool company will endorse the series of notes to the forfaiter. They will be endorsed *without recourse* thereby creating a forfaiting transaction. Together with any supporting documentation the series of promissory notes can then be sent by the exporter to the forfaiter.

A few further actions (detailed on the next page) need to be confirmed and authorized before the notes are discounted by the forfaiter.

❏ **The signatures on the notes and any other documentation needs to be confirmed as to their authenticity and validity.** This would usually be undertaken by the forfaiter, who can obtain authorized signatory lists from the Liverpool and Gdansk companies and the avalizing bank. Or, less likely, by the exporter's house bank, provided the exporter's house bank's confirmation is in a form that if one of the signatures invalidates the notes then the forfaiter can litigate against the exporter's house bank.

❏ **Clarification of any deductions to be made at maturity and who is to bear them.**

❏ **Check the validity and genuineness of the documents themselves.**

❏ **Other confirmations may be required depending on the actual documentation involved in each transaction.**

The forfaiter on receipt of the authorized and dated promissory notes and all confirmations will discount them at the previously agreed rate and send the net payout value to the Liverpool company.

The Liverpool company having endorsed the promissory notes, "without recourse" and now having shipped the machinery parts and received payment has no further liabilities either actual or contingent on the bill to the holders or future holders of the notes. It is not only the lack of contingent liabilities on the bill but the relative speed and flexibility that has been one reason for the increased use of forfaiting in certain market conditions. The Liverpool company may continue to have obligations to the Gdansk company depending on the terms of the sales contract. However, these are independent of and abstracted from the Gdansk company's and its avalizing bank's obligations to the promissory note holders. It is quite usual for the forfaiter or note holder to confirm to the underlying bank that they are holding promissory notes (amount, currency, maturity date) avalized by them. The forfaiter can now decide whether to hold these medium-term, bank avalized, fixed interest notes to maturity or to sell them to another holder. The sourcing of primary market paper is a key element in the forfaiting market.

In this example the forfaiter has directly contacted the exporter. However, there is no reason why the request to the forfaiter shouldn't come from the importer or any one of the house banks or even the avalizing bank. But the usual point of origination of primary forfaiting transactions, is as in this case, between the exporter and the forfaiter.

The Liverpool company is now looking for its next sales contract having shipped and been paid for the Gdansk sales contract.

Just to complete the picture, Figure 6.1 (page 57) shows how the promissory note may be sold between holders in the secondary market.

ELEVEN
A case study

In writing this case study I have outlined the underlying trade transaction and the financing of the transaction and then considered the detail and perspectives of each party. The case study is based on an actual example, although the names have been changed.

As the example in the previous chapter used a UK exporter, this case study is based on a German exporter and details the transaction between the German exporter's bank selling the payment obligation of the importer on to a forfaiter in the secondary market.

The underlying trade transaction (Figure 1.1) concerns a German engineering company, Deutsche Maschinen Fabrik GmbH (DMF) selling two paper machines to a Brazilian printing company, Industria Grafica Brasilia LDTA (IG Brasilia).

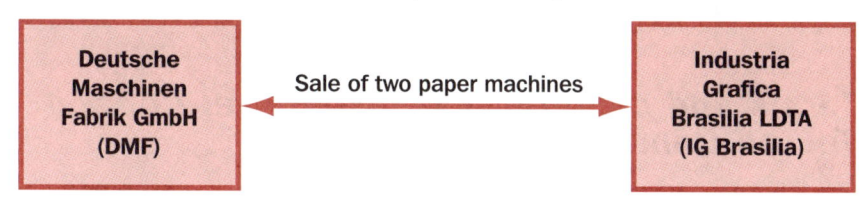

Figure 11.1 The underlying trade.

Teuton Bank are acting as bankers to the German exporters DMF. Teuton Bank are arranging the deferred payment promissory notes with the Brazilian importer IG Brasilia who have obtained the guarantee of Brasilia Bank. Brasilia Bank have agreed to put their aval on the promissory notes.

Teuton Bank will buy the promissory notes from DMF and then wish to sell these promissory notes and have contacted a potential purchaser Aval Co.

Figure 11.2 details the relationship of the participants in this transaction at the point in time when Teuton Bank contacts Aval Co.

Teuton Bank offers on 28 May 1996 to Aval Co. (a finance house that trades in forfaiting assets) the following deal on the telephone with the following terms and conditions for one of its customers, DMF. It is unlikely at this time the name of the customer would be revealed to Aval Co.

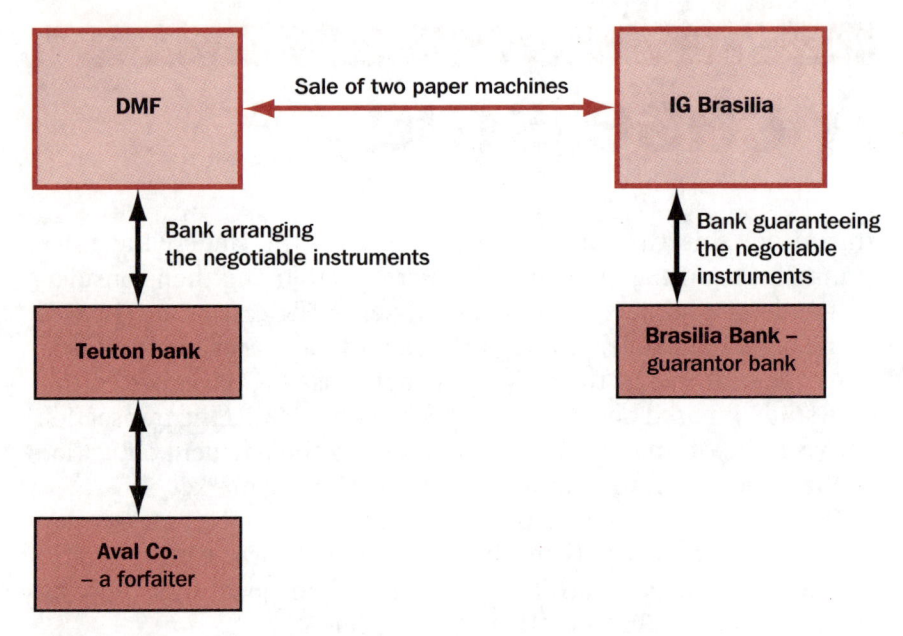

Figure 11.2 The underlying promissory note transaction.

Terms and conditions between Aval Co. and Teuton Bank

Amount:	DM2,300,000 approximately, including interest
Period:	five years
Importer:	Industria Grafica Brasilia, Ldta
Documentation:	ten semi-annual promissory notes, guaranteed per aval by Brasilia Bank, first maturity end of December 1996
Underlying transaction:	two paper machines
Discount under reserve:	latest by 30 August 1996
Delivery:	by end of June 1996
Availability of clean documents:	one month prior to first maturity
Semi-annual discount to yield:	7% per annum
Grace days:	15 per maturity
Commitment fee:	2% per annum, quarterly in advance, *pro rata temporis* from date of commitment until date of discount.

A deal between Aval Co. and Teuton Bank is verbally agreed and this is followed up on 29 May 1996 by an authorized fax from Teuton Bank detailing the terms and conditions of the deal. On the same day Aval Co. send an authorized fax (tested telex) with details of the transaction as a firm offer for the non-recourse purchase of the Teuton Bank transaction. There is also an attached statement of additional documentation which is required for Brazilian transactions. The firm offer is valid until 14.00 German time the following day.

The offer, with the associated terms and conditions, is accepted within the time limit subject to documentation and the deal is done on 30 May 1996.

At this stage it is quite possible the two paper machines haven't even been built, but the exporting company will by now know how much cash it will receive from Teuton Bank on despatch of the two machines to the Brazilian buyer.

It may be useful to identify the roles and objectives of each of the parties to this transaction at this juncture.

Deutsche Maschinen Fabrik GmbH (DMF)

DMF the German paper machine manufacturer has signed a sales contract for two of its paper machines to the Brazilian buyer. In order to make the sale DMF has arranged a credit finance package through its house bank, Teuton Bank. The importer has undertaken to meet the ten equal semi-annual notes to an invoice total of DM2,300,000.00 and provide a satisfactory bank guarantee for the payments.

DMF wishes to sell its machines at the best price it can on the best terms in order to maximize the returns to its shareholders. DMF would probably prefer cash preshipment transaction. However, if this isn't a possibility then as long as DMF keeps to the terms and conditions of the sale contract and maintains the integrity of the documentation then as in this example it has two prime financial considerations.

❏ Of immediate concern to DMF is the actual sum DMF will receive from Teuton Bank on transfer of the documents. This cash sum, provided the terms and conditions and dates in the forfaiting agreement between Teuton Bank and DMF are met, will be the sum of the net present value of each of the discounted notes which is *DM1,878,298.31* (calculation on page 124). This then is the sum DMF will receive on despatch of the goods and is the net sales revenue.

❏ However, the aggregate sale price on the notes including the interest element is DM2,300,000. This is also important to DMF. If the Brazilian importer IG Brasilia considers this price to be not as competitive as DMF's rivals for the same sales contract, then DMF could have lost the sale.

Industria Grafica Brasilia (IG Brasilia)

IG Brasilia, the Brazilian paper machine importer has signed a contract with the German machine manufacturer for the purchase of two paper machines. IG Brasilia is a paper printing company. It has been looking to acquire two new paper machines for some time. The German manufacturer DMF has also obtained a period of credit such that IG Brasilia must pay six months after shipment of the machines DM230,000; and then every six months after that a further DM230,000; there are ten payments in all. IG Brasilia has also to pay a fee to Brasilia Bank who assessed IG Brasilia's ability to meet the payments. Brasilia Bank having assessed the credit standing of IG Brasilia and for a fee of 1.5% per annum from IG Brasili,. Brasilia Bank will pay the notes if IG Brasilia is unable to meet the notes on due date. As an aside, often the bank guaranteeing the importer's obligations will demand the full amount of the guaranteee up front from the importer.

IG Brasilia wishes to buy the machines at the best price it can on the best terms in order to maximize the returns to its shareholders. IG Brasilia could probably if they had been able to pay cash (from their own resources or borrowed the funds) have arranged a different and possibly better deal. However, if this isn't a possibility then if IG Brasilia makes the purchase as in this example, in addition to the practical and documentary considerations it has only one prime financial concern.

❏ Can IG Brasilia generate enough net revenue from the two new paper machines to meet the six monthly payments and the quarterly guarantee fee?

Brasilia Bank

Brasilia Bank, is the Brazilian bank that has guaranteed the payment of the notes should IG Brasilia be unable to meet the payments on due date. Brasilia Bank will have made an assessment on the credit standing of the importer. If Brasilia Bank considers that the importer represents an acceptable debt risk then they will guarantee the notes at a rate that reflects the extent of the risk Brasilia Bank believe they are exposed to when guaranteeing the notes.

Brasilia Bank is taking on its books a contingent liability and is not directly using up its balance sheet. Merchant banks or banks without a deposit-gathering network and limited balance sheet space understandably, under the right conditions, seek this type of fee-earning revenue. However, various central banking authorities often attach a risk weighting to contingent liabilities as well as the bank's assets, so limiting the amount of contingent liability business an individual bank can undertake.

Teuton Bank

Teuton Bank is the bank acting for and on behalf of the German paper machine manufacturer. This may be the house bank of the exporter or it may be a bank who is arranging the finance for the house bank. In our example it is both the house bank and the arranging bank. The German exporter has been Teuton Bank's client for a number of years.

Teuton Bank has undertaken to arrange the financing package. Teuton Bank was made aware at an early stage by the exporter of the discussions between themselves and the importer. Finance houses and banks like Teuton Bank are competing for this type of business and it is possible that the exporter has also contacted other providers of a range of financial instruments. Since the exporter, like Teuton Bank, is also in business to maximize the wealth of its shareholders over time and to look for the best finance package, Teuton Bank would outline to the exporter terms and conditions as described at the beginning of the example. Again as an aside, the earlier an exporter contacts the forfaiter, then the better the advice and guidance the forfaiter is able to offer the exporter.

The two crucial elements would be first that the guaranteeing bank would be acceptable to the eventual note holders and second that the actual net cash sum that the exporter would receive on despatch of the goods and transfer of documentation to Teuton Bank would make the transaction commercially viable. If, in this example, the exporters say they need to produce *DM1,878,298.31* (calculation on page 126) to give them an acceptable gross profit margin, Teuton Bank can work out the structure and the gross cost of the deal to the importer. Let us say the suggested terms and conditions are as outlined at the beginning of the example, with one exception that is the semi-annual discount to yield is 8% per annum. Provided these terms and conditions and dates are adhered to, then the exporter DMF knows they will receive DM1878,298.31.

Teuton Bank's dilemma, to hold or trade? Once this deal is closed with the exporter Teuton Bank has two options:

❏ do they wish to fund it and hold each note to maturity?
❏ or do they trade it on? (Hopefully at a profit.)

In this example Teuton Bank have decided to sell the transaction to Aval Co.

Teuton Bank contacted Aval Co. to discuss the terms and conditions for trading the paper, which are laid out at the beginning of the example, even before they had closed the deal with the exporter. One can also understand why Teuton Bank is unlikely at this stage to reveal the participants in the trade since there is nothing other than a sense of ethics to stop Aval Co. making a direct approach to the German exporter at a discount rate between 7 and 8%, which is Teuton Bank's turn on the deal (under market conditions at the time of writing this turn would be perceived as being on the high side). Again, it should be stressed, this is a professional market with a limited number of participants and there is an unwritten code of conduct that the participants, if they wish to be an acceptable name in the market over time, adhere to.

Aval Co.

Aval Co. is a forfaiter as well as an originator, in this example they are looking to add to their portfolio of assets. They may hold these assets to maturity or trade them on before maturity. At this stage Aval Co. is considering the transaction. A deal between Aval Co. and Teuton Bank is verbally agreed subject to documentation and this is followed up on 29 May 1996 by an authorized fax from Teuton Bank detailing the terms and conditions of the deal. Later, on the same day Aval Co. sends an authorized fax with details of the transaction as a firm offer for the purchase of the non-recourse promissory notes of Teuton Bank's client. There is also an attached statement of additional documentation, which is required for Brazilian transactions. The firm offer is valid until 14.00 German time the following day. The offer, with the associated terms and conditions, is accepted within the time limit and the transaction is closed.

Calculations on the discount date at 30 August 1996

❏ **Between Teuton Bank and Aval Co.**

The terms and conditions are as at the beginning of this chapter. The method of discounting (Chapter 4) is semi-annual discount to yield and the discounted cash flow formula (DCF) (Chapter 2) is used (December 31 is a bank holiday in Germany but to simplify the calculations this has not been taken into account in the following examples.) The formula is as follows:

$$A = P/(1+r)^t$$

where A is the present value, P is the face value, r is the discount rate and t is the semi-annual time period.

First promissory note: 30 August 1996 to 31 December 1996 = 123 days plus 15 days of grace = 138 days

$$A = 230{,}000/(1 + 0.07 \times 138/360)$$

$$A = 230{,}000/(1 + 0.0268333)$$

$$A = 223{,}989.61$$

Summary of calculations between Teuton Bank and Aval Co.

Number of bills	10		Commit date	30/05/96
Currency	DM		Disbursement date	30/08/96
Basis	355/360		Days of grace	15
LIBOR compound	Six-monthly		Yield semi-annual	7%

No.	Maturity date		Life days	Face value	Net value
1	31/12/96		138	230,000	223989.61
2	30/06/97		319	230,000	216,375.13
3	31/12/97		503	230,000	208,900.43
4	30/06/98		684	230,000	201,798.89
5	31/12/98		868	230,000	194,827.73
6	30/06/99		1049	230,000	188,204.60
7	31/12/99		1233	230,000	181,703.05
8	30/06/00		1415	230,000	175,492.85
9	31/12/00	+1 day	1600	230,000	169,398.37
10	30/06/01	+2 days	1782	230,000	163,608.70
				2,300,000	**1,924,299**

Between exporter DMF and Teuton Bank

The terms and conditions are identical to those at the beginning of this chapter with the exception of the semi-annual discount rate which is now 8%.

$$A = P/(1+r)^t$$

where A is the present value, P is the face value, r is the discount rate and t is the semi-annual time period.

First note: 30 August 1996 to 31 December 1996 = 124 days plus 15 = 139 days

$$A = 230{,}000/(1 + 0.08) \times 138/360$$

$$A = 230{,}000/(1 + 0.0306666)$$

$$A = 223{,}156$$

Each note's present value (PV) is calculated as at 30 August 1996 giving the series aggregate PV. In this instance it is *DM1,878,298.31*.

Summary of calculations between Teuton Bank and DMF

Number of bills	10	Commit date	30/05/96
Currency	DM	Disbursement date	30/08/96
Basis	365/360	Days of grace	15
LIBOR compound	Six-monthly	Yield semi-annual	8%

No.	Maturity date	Life days		Face value	Net value
1	31/12/96		138	230,000	223,156.53
2	30/06/97		319	230,000	214,528.64
3	31/12/97		503	230,000	206,100.51
4	30/06/98		684	230,000	198,132.05
5	31/12/98		868	230,000	190,348.09
6	30/06/99		1049	230,000	182,988.67
7	31/12/99		1233	230,000	175,799.64
8	30/06/00		1415	230,000	168,966.26
9	31/12/00	+1 day	1600	230,000	162,293.16
10	30/06/01	+2 day	1782	230,000	155,984.76
				2,300,000	**1,878,298**

Commitment fee between Teuton Bank and Aval Co.

Looking at the commitment fee element Teuton Bank have undertaken to pay a commitment fee of 2% per annum quarterly in advance *pro rata temporis* from the date of Aval Co.'s commitment to the date of the discount under reserve calculation. Aval Co. invoice Teuton Bank from 30/5/96 to 30/8/96 (92 days) at 2% per annum so that the commitment fee is as follows:

$$DM2,300,000 \times 2/100 \times 92/360 = DM11,755.55$$

Summary to date

Let us consider what is happening subject to no changes in the dates in the original terms and conditions. A sales contract has been signed. The exporter knows they will receive *DM1,878,298.31* in cash on despatch of goods and delivery of satisfactory documentation. The importer has been given credit terms and will have to meet ten notes of DM230,000 each, every six months from the date of bill of lading. In addition, the importer will pay the importer country bank a guarantee fee of 1.5% per annum quarterly in advance. The arranging bank Teuton Bank will pay the exporter *DM1,878,298.31* on delivery of satisfactory documentation and will immediately pass on the clean documentation to Aval Co. for *DM1,924,299.36* (the differential of DM46,001.05 being Teuton Bank's profit on this transaction). Teuton Bank will have paid DM11,755.55 to Aval Co. for their given commitment. Teuton Bank has probably passed on the commitment fee charge according to the to the terms and conditions between it and the exporter. Hopefully so far, so clear, but this example is taken from an actual case and when you are dealing with physical manufacturing and transportation, difficulties often occur. This example is no exception.

Production problems

According to the documentation, the two paper machines are to be dispatched by the end of June and the notes discounted under reserve (a peculiarity of the Brazilian market) by 30 August 1996 at the latest. The reserve in this case, demanded by Aval Co. is that the particular documentation required by the Brazilian authorities must be ready and clean documents available one month prior to the first maturity. However, there are problems in the machine production shop and the sales contract is to be delayed by about two months. This will have repercussions for the German manufacturer and the Brazilian importer.

The Brazilian importer may be able to terminate the underlying sales contract and litigate for damages arising, it will depend on the terms and conditions of the sales contract between the two parties. Or, as in this case, both parties agree to the deferred shipment date. Teuton Bank agreed with the German exporter after prior consent of Aval Co. to an extension for the presentation of documentation by two months, all other terms and conditions remaining unchanged in their respective agreements. Under the terms of its agreement with Teuton Bank, Aval Co. had the right to make a further commitment fee charge. They would also have the right to decline to extend or to vary the terms and conditions of the agreement.

The point should be emphasized here that the forfaiting market is characterized by its flexibility, which is a major factor in its usefulness to exporters, to adjust to the underlying changes, delays and deferments often encountered in the production of capital goods and their transportation. It should be noted that the forfaiting contract is absolutely abstracted from any problems associated with the underlying sales contract. However, if the underlying terms and conditions are changed; such that, as in this case, the shipment date is altered, then the present value of the promissory note will need to be recalculated to the new value date based on the maturity date which will be altered in accordance with the new shipment date. In this particular case, when this calculation is made the present value received by the exporter could be DM1,844,000.

The two paper machines are shipped from Germany to Brazil on the 16 September 1996. A copy of the bill of lading, a copy of the commercial invoice from the German exporter to the Brazilian importer, the Brazilian import licence and authorization certificate and the ten avalized promissory notes are sent to Aval Co. by Teuton Bank. They agree a new value date of 30 September 1996 with calculation adjustments as necessary (all documentation is checked and authorized by both parties). As maturity dates are usually linked to the bill of lading the first maturity should now be the 16 March 1997.

These notes are discounted to net value as per the terms and conditions of the underlying contract between Aval Co. and Teuton

Bank and funds remitted to the bank net of the increased commitment fee charge.

Aval Co. – to hold or to trade?

Aval Co., like Teuton Bank before them, must decide:

❏ Do they wish to fund the notes and hold each note to maturity?
❏ or decide to do nothing now and look at it on an on-going basis?
❏ or do they want to trade the notes on? (Hopefully at a profit.)

In this example Aval Co. decide to hold the notes to maturity.

Aval Co. hold to maturity

When Aval Co. agreed to purchase this deal from Teuton Bank on 30 May 1996 it was subject to documentation satisfactory to Aval Co. The documentation included an unconditional, without deduction and irrevocable intention to pay at maturity date from Brasilia Bank and the address and place of domicile of payment. In the case of this transaction the payment was to be at the Brasilia bank. It was also agreed that clean documents were to be available one month prior to the first maturity. In the event, clean documentation was obtained by Aval Co. well before this date. It is industry practice to send for payment, i.e. collection on the documentation at least one month prior to the maturity date. The first maturity date of the first note in this case was the 31 December 1996 (although with the delay this would have been calculated to 16 March 1997). It is also standard practice for the buyer of the promissory notes to receive confirmation from the guarantor prior to payment when purchasing the notes.

When Aval Co. send the note for collection in late February 1997, they will receive confirmation from Brasilia Bank of the payment to be made on 16 March 1997. Brasilia Bank in turn would have collected the funds from the Brazilian importer. The remaining notes in the series will be collected in a similar manner unless Aval Co. decides to on sell the notes to another holder.

TWELVE

What next?

12.1 Background update
12.2 Forfaiting as a short-term trade instrument
12.3 Forfaiting as a financial instrument
12.4 Legal concerns
12.5 Taxation issues
12.6 Definition revisited

12.1 Background update

Forfaiting evolved in the 1950s using established trade negotiable instruments with the additional non-recourse characteristic. This created both liquidity in the asset structure of German manufacturing companies and removed the possibility of contingent liabilities that may have crystallized on the balance sheets of the mainly Swiss, German and Italian financial entities that discounted and then traded the non-recourse trade-related paper evidencing the underlying obligation of the importer.

In this kerbside free market there is some discussion as to the first non-recourse trade transaction. Did it revolve around Canadian blankets exported to Poland in 1949? Or French capital goods exported to Suez in 1956? And were the German manufacturers initially merely trying to sell on the political risk as they were uncertain of the goodwill of the Russian and East European buyers and preferred to trade through a neutral intermediary? Or was the West German manufacturers' primary concern not so much related to balance sheet liquidity, since the deposit taking West German banks had considerable equity stakes in these manufacturing companies, but rather reducing the potential political risk on their east European trade assets? What is not disputed, however, is that the growth of non-recourse financing was stimulated by virtue of the east European and Russian banks meeting their obligations on due date and then more recently, to the exporter's appetite for the flexibility of the instrument and the clean, non-recourse nature of this type of financing.

There are now a well-established primary and secondary forfaiting markets which in effect securitize the receivables of the exporting company. The limited empirical evidence available would suggest that there has been an underlying growth in the primary market.

This may be attributed to the following factors:

1 Exporters are increasingly familiar with forfaiting and being able to offer credit to buyers and potential buyers has always been a selling point.
2 Forfaiting can be used within a free market and has a flexibility that government export credit agency sponsored schemes may not have. Driven by the profit motive and a need to maximize shareholder's wealth, forfaiters will try and adapt the forfaiting terms and conditions to suit both the exporters' and importers' needs.
3 In the normal course of business there is no recourse to previous holders or the exporter by the holder at maturity if the negotiable instrument is not met at maturity. Once the sale has been made the exporter takes the money and moves on to the next trade.
4 It should be mentioned with reference to **3**, that although the forfaiting contract will be abstracted from the sales contract terms and conditions, there may be recourse on the forfaiting contract if lack of due diligence or fraud can be proven.
5 Forfaiting practitioners have now been knocking on doors, speaking at trade shows and generally contacting exporters for some 35 years to find out if this is the appropriate credit finance for a potential client and then marketing its possibilities. In part the growth of the primary non-recourse market is a function of the familiarization of forfaiting with exporters.

The secondary market is also changing. At the time of writing there is probably more forfaiting paper in existence than at any other time. However, there appears to be less trading of this paper in the secondary market as the holders although they enjoy the ability to sell the instrument, increasingly appear to wish to hold the paper to maturity and live with the various holding risks.

Forfaiting has continued to evolve. As detailed above, in the primary market it has continued to be used in its classic form for medium-term funding of capital exports from industrialized countries to industrializing countries. The underlying receivable stream characteristically being evidenced by ten semi-annual notes guaranteed by a bank in the importers' country, are discounted at a fixed rate to their present value and crucially being without recourse by the holder in event of non-payment at maturity. However, in addition non-recourse financing has also evolved along two different routes.

❏ for funding short-term trade transactions (Section 12.2)
❏ as a financial rather than a trade instrument (Section 12.3)

12.2 Forfaiting as a short-term trade instrument

This variation of the classic forfaiting transaction may not be such a variant as to be worthy of special mention. It could be said to be merely another example of the flexibility of forfaiting. The adding of a non-recourse element to the financing of a six-month deferred payment letter of credit for oil, grain or other commodity exports is a relatively recent change in direction. It is based on the same reasons of market need as generated the capital market instrument in the 1960s.

Figure 12.1 shows a German coffee trader, buying on the London coffee market and then selling the physical coffee to a Croatian

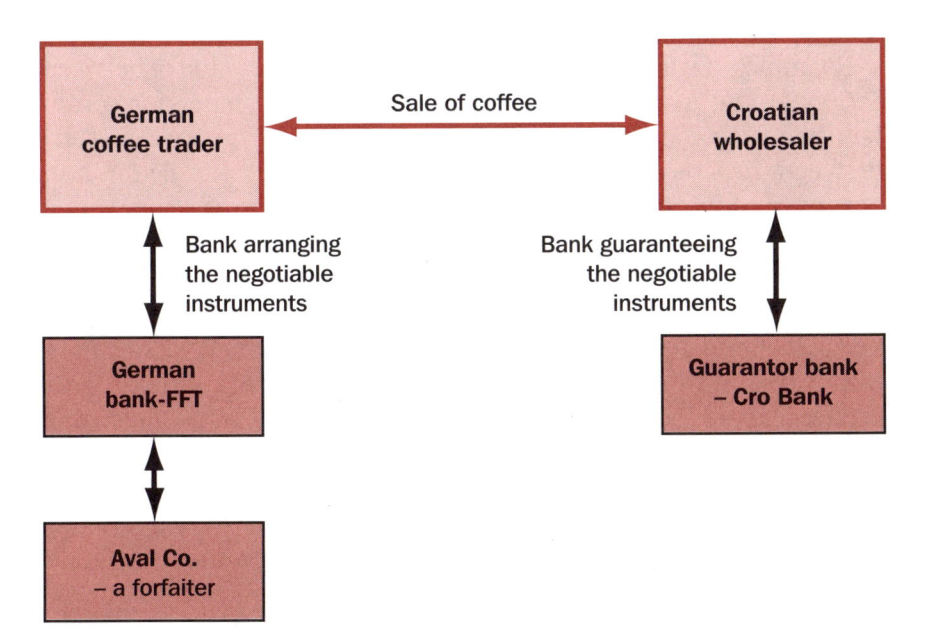

Figure 12.1 The underlying negotiable instrument six-month coffee trade transaction.

wholesaler/retail chain. The German coffee trader needs cash to meet cash obligations to the London Commodity Exchange. The Croatian wholesaler wants six month's credit. Cro Bank likes the credit risk of the Croatian importer and can augment its fee income. The German coffee trader likes the idea of non-recourse finance if the negotiable instrument is not met at maturity in six months time.

German Bank-FFT organizes the non-recourse negotiable instrument and knows that forfaiter Aval Co. will take the six-month Cro Bank risk.

The payment element of this transaction will be evidenced by one note, although if the transaction size is equal to a container ship of coffee of say $10 million, there may be ten notes each with a face value of $1 million, which are probably easier to sell on by German Bank-FFT than one note for $10 million. Because of the relatively short time span these notes are unlikely to be as remunerative to the forfaiter as the classic five-year capital goods transaction. Also, because of time constraints they are much less likely to be sold on more than once in the secondary market.

As with all free-market forfaiting transactions, there is no publicity attached to these short-term commodity transactions as the nature of the private trade deal is between a bank and its customer. So again it is not possible to quantify this expanding market.

Examples of such short-term deals could be in the value of between $500,000 and $10 million, for up to a six-month tenor for cotton between Ukraine and Slovakia, sugar from UK to Russia, steel between the Czech Republic and the UK and refined petroleum from France to Morocco.

12.3 Forfaiting as a financial instrument

The use of non-recourse trade paper as a purely financial instrument rather than a negotiable trade credit, be it for the classic five-year capital export or a six-month commodity credit, may present a change in how forfaiting paper is perceived by all the parties to the trade or financial transaction and the respective state, taxation and legal authorities.

Firstly let us look at the mechanics of the non-recourse obligation as a financial instrument. Let us go back to the classic forfaiting deal in figure 12.2, using the same example as in Section 9.6.

We know that in this example Newcastle Engineering (NE) wants to make a sale to Indonesian Importer (II) and get paid. NE can be

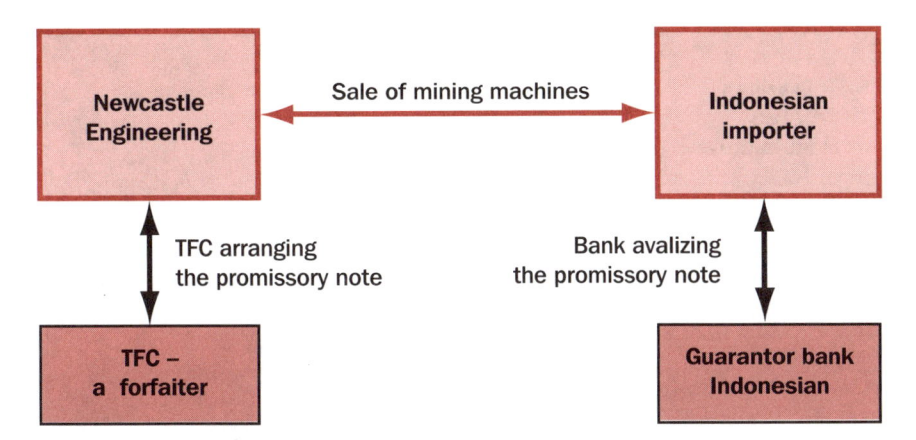

Figure 12.2 The underlying promissory note transaction – classic forfaiting deal.

paid in a variety of ways, such as open market operations, cash in advance or on invoice, a sight letter of credit, non-recourse promissory notes or through a government export scheme.

Let us say NE decides in this particular set of circumstances that it is most appropriate to use an Export Credit Guarantee Department (ECGD) facility organized by their clearing bank. Most western governments will operate some form of credit assistance/guarantee for the supplier in order to encourage their domestic industry to export.

II is lent 85% of the hard currency funds to meet the invoice and they must provide the balance from their own resources, either by drawing down cash from their assets or borrowing cash from their bankers. A way of meeting this 15% hard currency cash payment is for II to write a non-recourse promissory note which would generate as a minimum a present value equal to the 15% hard currency cash payment (tenor of from six months to five years) and have it guaranteed by an Indonesian bank, who add their aval to the promissory note. This note is then discounted by a bank or financial institution willing to take the tenor and the Indonesian bank guarantee risk. This is a non-recourse bank guaranteed negotiable instrument. There is an underlying trade but it is only indirectly linked to this particular promissory note. So is it a financial or a trade instrument? Does this make any difference? And if so to whom?

Before we consider these questions, let us review two other forms of non-recourse instruments as financial rather than trade instruments in Figure 12.3.

Forfaiting for exporters

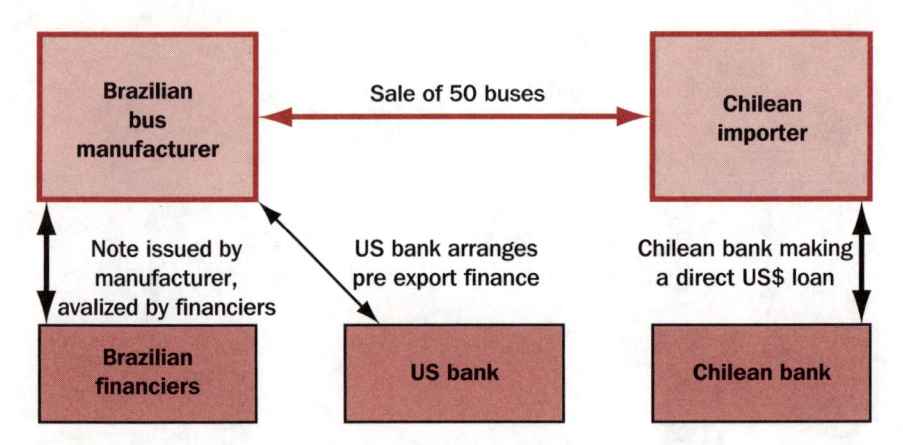

Figure 12.3 The underlying promissory note transaction – a financial rather than a trade instrument.

A Brazilian bus manufacturer wins a contract to supply 50 buses to a Chilean importer. Let us say in this instance a Chilean bank has agreed to make a direct US$ loan to the Chilean importer to pay for the buses. Terms have been agreed such that the Brazilian manufacturer will receive payment two months after delivery. In the meantime the Brazilian bus manufacturer has to meet its hard currency liabilities to its suppliers. The bus manufacturer has no hard currency or access to hard currency through its domestic financiers. The bus manufacturer requires short-term hard currency preshipment finance. The trade department of a US bank agrees with the Brazilian financiers to discount a non-recourse six-month promissory note issued by the Brazilian bus manufacturer and avalized by the Brazilian financiers. The US bank wants a non-recourse instrument so when it discounts the note it has no contingent liability. It is less clear cut whether this is a financial instrument or a trade-related instrument and in part will depend on the underlying documentation. In any event, as before, the same questions can be asked: is it a financial or a trade instrument? Does this make any difference and if so to whom?

There is another variation that could be provided using the example above, in that exactly the same instrument is arranged by the US bank for the Brazilian bus manufacturer avalized by the Brazilian financiers. There is, however, no underlying trade and the funds are used as working capital by the Brazilian bus manufacturers. This is self-evidently a non-recourse financial and not a trade instrument, avalized by a Brazilian financial institution.

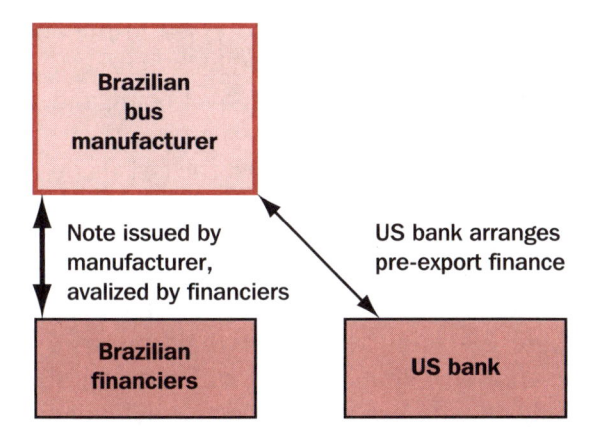

Figure 12.4 The underlying promissory note transaction – a financial instrument.

As in the previous examples, the same questions can be asked. If these are financial instruments evidencing a receivable rather than a trade instrument evidencing a receivable, does this make any difference? And if so to whom? These questions are considered in the section "Trade versus financial instrument" (page 139).

12.4 Legal concerns

In Chapter 7 we looked at documentation and briefly considered some of the legal concerns associated with the instruments used to evidence non-recourse transactions from the perspective of a "how to" guide, which is the book's main purpose.

There is considerable scope to write a legal treatise on the actual and potential legal implications of the non-recourse instruments used to evidence forfaiting transactions. Forfaiting uses a variety of negotiable instruments, crosses ill-defined areas of legal jurisdiction and has a dynamic flexibility as regards the underlying and changing terms and conditions and nature of its use. In response to the questions posed in Section 12.3, and as a minimum it would seem appropriate at least to air certain legal aspects of forfaiting.

Jurisdiction

If momentarily we consider the examples given so far in this chapter, the first question to arise for the plaintiff would be under which legal jurisdiction and in which country should their grievance be heard. It is possible that this point may be addressed in the documentation, if a negotiable instrument is used which has a side agreement/guarantee attached. However with an aval being added to the note, the note is highly unlikely to specify such detail.

Common-sense would at first suggest the jurisdiction would be the country of the importer or obligor. However, the holder of the note may be more familiar with the legal systems and structures of the exporter country. The prospective plaintiff would have to make a case why the jurisdiction would be in the exporter's country and why the case should be conducted under that country's legal system. Whether the courts of that country will accept jurisdictions may depend entirely on whether the prospective defendant can be made subject to the orders of the court. Application can be made to the court for permission to "serve out of jurisdiction", and such applications may be refused by the court.

Code Napoleon

English law recognizes the endorsement of documentation although the aval is not part of English law. It is also part of English law that the forgery of an endorsement breaks the chain of liability. It also has yet to be proven under English law that the signatory of an avalized instrument has the same legal obligations as the endorsement of a bill or note. "Aval" is not mentioned in the Bills of Exchange Act 1882, but it has found its way more and more into use in this country and one now regularly sees the main clearing banks guaranteeing bills of exchange "good for aval". Under the Code Napoleon writing *per aval* or *without recourse* on a promissory note confers an obligation on the avalizor, abstracted from any underlying trade contract. However, under Article 9 of the International Convention for Commercial Bills (Geneva Convention, 1930), the drawer of a bill will still under this article be bound by his obligation as the drawer of the bill. A separate written undertaking attached to the bill of exchange to the effect that the forfaiter will not take any action against the drawer in the event of the bill not being met at maturity has to date never been legally tested. It is also part of the same Geneva Convention that the forgery of an aval will not affect liability (Article 32: "the aval is valid even when the liability which he has guaranteed is inoperative for any reason, other than defect of form"). Again it is worth mentioning that the UK was not a signatory to the 1930 Geneva Convention.

Documentation differences

Each set of documents, setting aside the jurisdiction or legal system, evidencing the underlying trade or financial transaction is likely to be subject to a variety of legal precedents relating to the bills, notes or the style of the particular negotiable instrument, or the type of guarantee. In certain cases there are specific statutes that relate to the law governing forfaiting transactions. However, most precedents or laws relating to the negotiable instruments are by assumed association rather than by particular and direct reference. Nor can we fall back on the potential comfort of practical intent of the parties or general guidelines, since it is possible that if local regulations or laws as regards documentation have not been correctly applied, then it is feasible that the documents evidencing the underlying trade could be deemed to be null and void.

1. Trade versus financial instrument

With regard to the questions posed at the end of Section 12.3, it is clear that trade-backed negotiable instruments tend to be held in higher regard by parties to the transaction and by the regulatory authorities than financial negotiable instruments. The reasons for this are not ill-founded, being mainly generated by precedent. The syndicated loan and sovereign debt financial market of the 1970s resulted in a huge free transfer of funds from the northern to the southern hemispheres. The legacy of this and the prejudices it generated in all parties will take some time to erase. The clichéd view of funds from oil surplus countries being channelled by western banks into grandiose projects and private bank accounts has more than a ring of truth to it. What was certain was that the borrowing countries carried enormous debts into the future with large interest payments for little obvious tangible benefit. However, trade debt relating to specific consumption or investment goods could be readily identified and in some countries a tiering of payment obligations took place. Although it wasn't always the case, meeting trade debt obligations often took precedence over the financial debt obligations of the borrowing country. In the majority of instances of general debt rescheduling in the 1980s the debtor countries would often exclude trade credits involving the import, pre-export or export of tangible goods across international borders.

It is probably this legacy and pragmatism that has given trade-related negotiable instruments a higher standing than purely financial obligations. At the time of writing the majority by value and number, of forfaiting transactions are trade related. However, there is a growth in the instrument being either a hybrid or a pure financial instrument. It is beholden on all parties relating to transactions in the secondary market to identify the underlying nature of the obligation. Non-recourse trade-related paper will probably carry a different perceived credit risk than non-recourse financial paper and this will be reflected in the credit risk element of the discount rate used in each case.

2. Primary versus secondary market

Section 3.8 defined and looked at the detail of the primary and secondary markets. However, in this brief legal glance at these two markets the point should be made that the legal obligations and market expectations, in spite of the non-recourse nature of the instrument, are placed largely on the shoulders of the primary forfaiter. There is a minimum level of due diligence which if not exercised by the primary forfaiter would leave the primary forfaiter open to recourse by a following trader in the same instrument. The point of potential contention and difference is, of course, defining the minimum level of expected due diligence of the primary forfaiter. The onus of responsibility is practical rather than legal and is enhanced by the need for flexibility and speed of transactions that are characteristics that have always been associated with forfaiting. The primary forfaiter will usually not reveal the name of the exporter to potential purchasers and will jealously guard the relationship with the client. In these sort of circumstances the following purchaser has a right to expect a considerable degree of diligence from the primary forfaiter. However, this does not absolve the secondary market trader from their responsibility to buy and sell the negotiable instrument such that they are selling a future valid claim which can be related to a *bona fide* transaction.

12.5 Taxation issues

In Chapter 9 we saw that the accounting treatment of potential revenue and/or cost streams over a number of accounting periods and the subjective valuation of assets as at the balance sheet date allows accounting entities, subject to consistency, objectivity, entity, prudence, in the UK the Accounting Standards Boards' Statements of Standard Accounting Practice (SSAP) and Financial Reporting Statements (FRS) and the taxation statutes, to shift accounting losses or profits across accounting periods. The Inland Revenue and any state tax-raising entity will take the trading profit or loss of an entity over an accounting period but then adjust it to establish the taxable profit or loss for that accounting period. Specific bad debts and general bad debt provisions, depreciation and capital allowances, stock equalization and deferred tax adjustments, the use of actual interest paid and received as against accrued income will be dealt with by the Inland Revenue or any tax authorities as would be applied to any financial instrument and entity. Forfaiting will be handled no differently to any other negotiable instrument. What may cause tax authorities to act in a different manner as regards the tax treatment of forfaiting paper is not so much the negotiable instrument but the nature of the business of the underlying entity. Is it the intention of that entity to hold the negotiable instrument to maturity or has the negotiable instrument been purchased with the intention of trading the paper before its maturity date?

In the UK, the House of Lords decision (Willingale *v* International Commercial Bank, 1978) was that the discount on a forfaiting instrument is not liable to tax until it has actually been received at maturity date, even though the revenue stream on the negotiable instrument may have been apportioned over the lifetime of that instrument until its maturity date. This applies to an investing entity whose initial intention is to hold the instrument to maturity. However, if it is the intention to trade the instrument then if the purchase and sale is within the trading period there is no problem since there is an in and out price. If, however, the note is held over an accounting period, the accounting and tax treatment may be at odds, but presently there is no specific legal precedent. However, provided the entity is consistent, it may apply the 1978 House of Lords decision.

12.6 Definition revisited

If the classic non-recourse (forfaiting) trade transaction is defined by its characteristics, then as first detailed in Chapter 1, let us return to that definition:

> Non-recourse trade finance is a free-market, medium-term trade credit, for capital goods, arranged by a western manufacturer to an importer in an industrializing country which has limited access to hard currency. The trade credit is without recourse, fixed rate, usually bank guaranteed and is often evidenced by a series of negotiable bills of exchange or promissory notes repayable semi-annually.

Perhaps the most relevant characteristic and the reason for use of non-recourse finance is its flexibility both to adapt to current market requirements and to make use of existing finance instruments, this makes any definition based on its characteristics at a point in time difficult to support. To illustrate this let's reconsider the above definition.

Free market – this is undoubtedly a free-market instrument although it is sometimes used by state export credit agencies, for example, Mediocredito Centrale SpA.

Medium term – although historically the term has been up to five years, increasingly non-recourse financing is being used for six months (or shorter) receivable financing.

Trade credit – although historically there has been an underlying trade funded by the credit, non-recourse financing is now being used to evidence purely financial obligations.

Capital goods – although historically the funding has been for capital goods, non-recourse financing is now being used to fund commodity trades.

Western manufacturer – as the nature of the instrument has changed and the credit standing of various countries has improved forfaiting's geographic spread has become increasingly diverse.

Importer in an emerging/industrializing country – this has been and is probably a constant. Although one is continually surprised at the use of forfaiting to finance exports to industrialized countries. There are other methods of paying for goods and if the importer has hard currency liquidity, there is less need for credit to be supplied by the seller. If credit is required it can be provided by direct funding in the importers country.

Without recourse – this is not the umbrella defence it may appear to be. It has yet to be rigorously tested in any legal case. In any event the "correct" jurisdiction and legal system are fertile ground for discussion, as are the potentially different obligations of both the primary and secondary forfaiter. However, from a practical standpoint with forfaiting there is no contingent liability on the exporter, or holder in due course.

Fixed rate – if the importer wants floating rate, it can be arranged.

Bank guaranteed – the majority of non-recourse paper is still bank guaranteed.

A series of negotiable instruments – the tenor, the face value of the bills of exchange or promissory notes, size and the number of bills/notes can be varied as appropriate to the client's requirements.

Promissory notes – any form of negotiable instrument evidencing the underlying debt can be used. The legal standing of each type of instrument will vary within legal boundaries and will certainly vary across legal boundaries.

Semi-annually – the repayment of a note in a series of notes is again a variable that can be adapted to the importer's requirements.

Forfaiting, because of its flexibility, is difficult to define and this combined with its private, free-market publicly unlisted nature, also makes it difficult to quantify.

However, forfaiting, even with its attendant definition and quantification problems and potential legal, taxation and accounting interpretations has now however matured into an integral part of the market for debt.

However forfaiting's flexibility to changing market requirements and the pragmatism of its practitioners may create definition and quantifications problems, but will probably ensure that this non-recourse trade/financial instrument will be used increasingly in the future.

Glossary

Note: Terms used in forfaiting parlance, do not always correspond with their use in other financial markets.

Annual discount to yield. Takes into account the time value of money and is the compounded per annum discount rate, divided into the face value of the promissory note. For example a note, face value in three years time of 100, with an annual discount to yield of 10% per annum has a present value of 75.13 (100/1.331).

Aval. Inseparable from the financial instrument and effectively gives a guarantee and is abstracted from the performance of the underlying trade contract. Article 31 of the 1930 Geneva Convention on Bills of Exchange says that the "aval" can be written on the bill itself or on an "allonge". In certain countries an aval may have an indeterminate legal status and a guarantee may be used as an alternative. The guarantor per aval is a primary obligor.

Avalizor. The person, bank (usually) or financial entity who give the aval.

Bill of exchange. A negotiable instrument which is drawn on the importer/obligor by the exporter and accepted by the importer/obligor and returned to the exporter as the payment mechanism for the underlying obligation of the Importer. Value can be transferred by endorsement. The addition "without recourse" is affixed to endorsements and this waives the payment obligation of the endorser. The market, through the use of a waiver, acts as if the exporter is not liable as drawer.

Bill of lading. Bills of lading are pieces of paper which are issued when goods are loaded on a vessel based on a contract between the shipper and the exporter. This document conveys all rights to the shipped goods by its bearer.

Burgschaft. This is similar to a letter of guarantee, historically used in central Europe, crucially it is not abstracted from but dependent on the satisfactory fulfilment of the underlying transaction.

Certificate of inspection. Some countries and purchasers may require a certificate of inspection, usually given by an accredited third party, confirming the specifications of the goods shipped.

Certificate of origin. Certain countries require a signed statement as to the origin of the export item.

Coface. The French ECA.

Commercial invoice. The commercial invoice is a bill for the goods from the exporter to the importer. A commercial invoice will include basic information about the transaction.

Commitment fee. The fee charged for the commitment period by the forfaiter and paid by the exporter (or seller in the secondary market) subject to the terms and conditions of the forfaiting contract.

Commitment period. From the date of signing of the forfaiting contract between the exporter/seller of paper and the forfaiter and the value date.

Commitment. An obligation on both the forfaiter and the exporter to stand by the terms and conditions of a forfaiting contract signed by them.

Contingent liability. A potential liability which crystallizes into an actual liability on an entity's balance sheet when the original third party or parties have failed to meet their obligations and the entity then has to take the place and obligations of the original obligor(s).

Counter-party. An entity selling/buying assets/obligations with another entity.

Credit margin. That part of the discount rate over and above the cost of funding. The credit margin will reflect the perceived credit risk of the importer/guarantor and its country for the respective credit period.

Days of grace. Additional days added to the time period of the obligation to take into account, through experience, settlement delays associated with certain countries and or guaranteeing/avalizing banks.

Derivative hedge. An instrument derived from the underlying asset market which can act in an opposite manner to that fixed asset market and in so doing can lock into an asset (interest or exchange rates) position at that point in time, so removing interest rate or exchange rate risk.

Discount rate. The rate at which the face value of the bill or note is discounted to its present value. It is composed of an objective cost of carry for the period (such as LIBOR) and a margin for the perceived credit risk of the obligor/guarantor.

Documentary collection. The process of delivering title, shipping and related documents for the goods exported.

ECA. Export credit agencies are state bodies or institutions for assisting exporters in industrialized countries sell their goods by guaranteeing the credit payment (in part or in full) in industrializing countries.

ECGD. Export Credit Guarantee Department, the British ECA.

Exim. The United States of America and Japan and others, ECA

Export licence. Exporters in certain countries are required by their government or state bodies to obtain an export licence. This often relates to certain types of goods or the purchasing country.

Face value. The value shown on a promissory note or bill of exchange and is the amount due at maturity.

Factoring. A method for generating cash to an entity from its short term receivables, under the terms and conditions of an agreement between the entity and the factorer. These terms and conditions may leave the factorer with recourse to the entity in event of default. The entities receivables are not evidenced by a negotiable instrument but usually by invoices.

Forfaiter (primary). An individual or financial entity that arranges a forfaiting contract directly with an exporter and then holds or sells on the payment obligations of the importer/guarantor.

Forfaiter (secondary). An individual or financial entity that buys (other than from the exporter) or sells the payment obligations of the importer/guarantor.

Guarantee fee. A sum paid by the importer, usually as a percentage per annum of the average face value of the bills or notes outstanding, to the avalizing/guaranteeing bank.

Guarantee. A letter of guarantee is a document signed by the guarantor in which the guarantor, abstracted from the underlying sales contract, commits themselves absolutely to pay a series of promissory notes or bills of exchange on due date if the obligor fails to make payment due at maturity.

Guaranteeing/avalizing bank. The person, bank or financial entity who gives the guarantee for the importer.

Hermes. The German ECA.

Import licence. Importers in certain countries are required by their government or state bodies to obtain an import licence, usually allocating foreign exchange to future payment obligations.

Insurance certificate. If the seller provides insurance, the insurance certificate states the amount and type of cover.

Interest rate risk. Promissory notes and bills of exchange in their usual form have a face value reduced by the discount rate for the tenor of the period of the note to their present value. This means the instrument is a fixed rate instrument and if the holder does not match the funding period or buy a derivative hedge then they will carry an interest rate risk.

LIBOR. London Interbank Offered Rate, the free market objective interest rate at which banks offer funds to other banks of a certain perceived market standing.

Maturity date. The date of the payment obligation. The holder will often have sent (presented) the relevant bill or note up to four weeks prior to the maturity date to the avalizing or guaranteeing entity for payment.

Mediocredito SpA. State-owned export agency.

Negotiable instrument. A written financial undertaking by means of which ownership to a future obligation can be transferred between two parties, usually by endorsement.

Non-recourse debt. See without-recourse debt.

Option fee. The fee covering an option period charged by the forfaiter and paid by the exporter subject to terms and conditions of the forfaiting contract.

Option period. From the date of signing of the forfaiting contract, to either the signing of the underlying trade contract or its frustration.

Option. An obligation on both the forfaiter and the exporter to stand by the terms and conditions of a forfaiting contract signed by them, provided that in due course the underlying sales contract between the exporter and the importer is signed.

Preshipment finance. Usually short-term funding to fund the inventory and production costs associated with manufacturing capital goods for export.

Promissory note. A negotiable instrument which is drawn/issued by the importer and accepted/taken by the exporter as the payment mechanism for the underlying obligation of the importer. Value can be transferred by endorsement. The addition of *without recourse* to each endorsement means the exporter and successive holders have no contingent liability.

Semi-annual discount to yield. Takes into account the time value of money and is the compounded semi-annual discount rate, divided into the face value of the promissory note. For example a note, face value in three years' time of 100, with a semi-annual discount to yield of 10% per annum has a present value of 74.62 (100/1.34).

Shipment date. The loading date on a vessel, airplane or truck. Also often the trigger date for setting the period to the maturity dates of the negotiable instrument(s).

Silent confirmation. This is in effect a counter-guarantee. Given by an entity outside the importer's country to the exporter usually on a sight letter of credit, without reference to the importer or importer's guarantor and is intended thereby to reduce the credit risk to the exporter.

Simple discount to yield. Takes into account the time value of money but is the uncompounded per annum discount rate, divided into the face value of the promissory note. For example a note, face value in three years' time of 100, with a simple discount to yield of 10% per annum has present value of 76.92 (100/1.30).

Stand-by letter of credit. This is a form of guarantee rather than a documentary letter of credit. It will often take the place of an aval if an aval is not legally recognized under a country's statute (e.g. USA). It is issued under the importer's instructions by a bank in favour of the beneficiary, it is irrevocable and unconditional subject to the presentation of certain documentation as defined in the stand by letter of credit.

Straight discount. Has nothing to do with the time value of money but is the *rate* applied to the face value of the promissory note. For example a note, face value in three years of 100, with a straight discount of 10% per annum has a present value of 70.

Tenor. Period of promissory note or bill of exchange from the issue date until its maturity date in the primary market, from the purchase/sale date to maturity in the secondary market.

Under reserve. Purchase of a debt obligation subject to the right to rescind the purchase if certain conditions are not met. These conditions are usually documentary such as to establish that the debt obligation being bought and sold is valid and legally binding on the issuer/guarantor.

Value date. The date to which the present value is calculated from the maturity date of a single or series of negotiable instruments, upon sale by one party to another, simply the date on which the purchase price for documents is being transferred.

Without-recourse debt. A debt obligation on which the right of recourse has been forfeited, in which a condition is added to the endorsement in order to protect the exporter and any subsequent sellers, if the instrument is not paid at maturity, by the original obligor.

APPENDIX
Approaches to calculating interest and discount rates

Introduction

It is hardly an exaggeration to say that trade finance, and particularly forfaiting is all about discounting of zero-coupon paper. The absence of a stream of payments in the form of interest or coupons, as would typically be found on interest-bearing instruments, imposes methodological constraints on discounting procedures. The purpose of this appendix is to discuss alternative methodologies for discounting, placing them into a coherent theoretical basis and to review approaches to quantifying yield curves, the key market input when discounting zero-coupon paper.

I would like to thank Dr Andrew Bagley for his contribution.

Compound interest

The calculation of compound interest is widely known and understood. The maturing payment of principal plus interest after n years is given by the expression

$$P + I = P(1 + i/m)^{mn} \qquad (1)$$

where P is the principal, I is the interest, i is the interest rate (in decimals) and m is the compounding frequency per annum.

As most practitioners will know, I increases as the compounding period becomes shorter. If we compare a compounding period of six months against 12 months for a one-year maturity and interest of

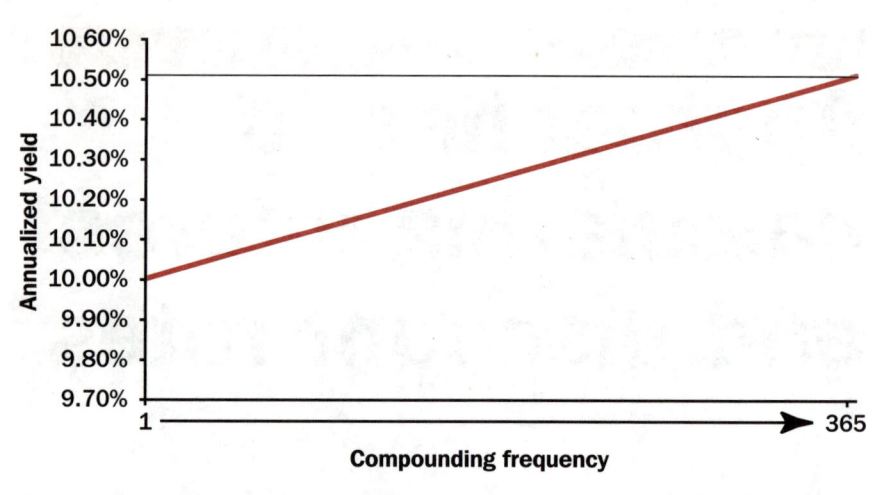

Figure A.1 Annualized yield versus compounding frequency.

10%, we find that whereas the discount to yield on the 12-month compounding is 10%, on the semi-annual compounding it is 10.25%. If we continue to use shorter and shorter compounding periods, we find that the annualized yield approaches a maximum value, in this case 10.5156% as we move to daily compounding (see Figure A.1).

As we increase compounding frequency to fractions of days, m tends to infinity and we approach a limit which is called continuous compounding. At this point, the continuously compounded rate (R) is given by

$$R = m \ln(1 + i/m) \qquad (2)$$

where m is the compounding frequency of the interest rate we are converting to continuous compounding, ln is the natural logarithm and the maturing payment is given by

$$P + I = P e^{Rn} \qquad (3)$$

where e is the natural constant 2.71828.

A continuously compounded interest rate can be converted into an annualized rate (or other basis) using the formula

$$i = m(e^{R/m} - 1)$$

Thus a continuously compounded 10% interest rate is equivalent to an annually compounded yield of 10.5171%, a figure fractionally higher than the 10.5156% found with daily compounding.

If we take our case described above, of 10% interest rate, compounded semi-annually, on £100, the maturing payment of principal plus interest after one year is £110.25. Calculating the continuously compounded rate equivalent to 10% semi-annual compounding:

$$R = 2 \ln (1 + 0.1/2) = 0.097580 = 9.758\%$$

and the maturing principal plus interest after one year is

$$P + I = 100 \, e^{0.09758 \times 1} = 110.25$$

Use of continuous compounding gives us tremendous flexibility in calculating face values and discounted values of zero coupon notes. Knowing the interest rate and basis of compounding enables us to use equation (2) above to convert to continuous compounding and equation (3) then enables us to calculate the face value directly.*

Discounting

Frequently in trade finance, we know the face value of a note, which represents principal plus interest payable at maturity, and our objective is to calculate its present value. Clearly, if a bank purchases the note, the purchase price must be financed until the note matures. The purchase price effectively becomes the principal of a loan and we can simply rearrange equation (1) above to calculate the principal which after financing costs will equal the maturing face value of the note $(P + I)$:

$$P = (P + I)/(1 + i/m)^{mn} \equiv [P + I][1 + i/m]^{-mn} \qquad (4)$$

Again, we can convert the factor $(1 + i/m)^m$, in equation (4) to a continuously compounded discounted factor using equation (2) and discount to find a present value using the expression

$$P = [P + I]e^{-Rn} \qquad (5)$$

---

*Alternatively, the expression $P + I = Pe^{R[t_1-t_0]/365}$ may be used, where t_1 and t_0 are the maturity date and today's date, respectively.

Zero-coupon yield curves

Conversion to continuous compounding offers major advantages in reducing the complexity of calculations. The other major input into calculating face values and discounted values is the zero-coupon yield curve.

We have already indicated that discounting in trade finance involves primarily the discounting of zero coupon paper. A bill of exchange is clearly a zero coupon document as there are no interim interest or principal payments prior to maturity. Forfaiting transactions can similarly be thought of as consisting of a series of zero coupon payments. Intuitively, it would therefore seem necessary to use a zero-coupon yield curve in determining discounted values and face values rather than a yield curve constructed on the basis of LIBOR rates or yields on gilt-edged stock involving periodic payments of interest.

Under normal circumstances, yield curves have the gradually upward sloping structure as shown in Figure A.2.

For upward sloping yield curves, the zero-coupon yield curve is always above the coupon-bearing yield curve. This is because on a coupon-bearing bond, the investor receives some payments (perhaps just interest) before maturity. For upward sloping yield curves, the discount rate on these prepayments is lower than for the final payment date and accordingly the overall yield on the bond is lower than for a zero coupon bond with a single payout corresponding to

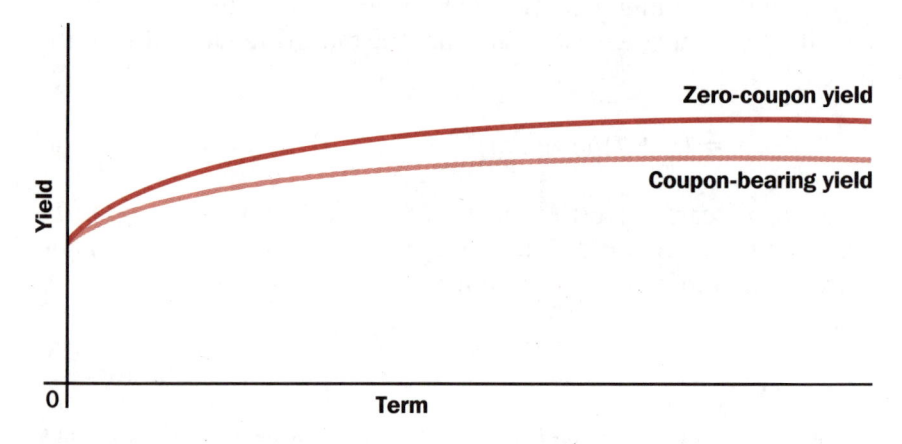

Figure A.2 The term structure of interest rates.

final maturity. If we were to use the yield curve for coupon-bearing bonds to calculate yields for zero coupon instruments, we would be understating the applicable rates.

In practice, zero coupon yields usually cannot be observed directly, and they must be inferred from the prices of coupon-bearing bonds. A commonly used method is the bootstrap technique. This involves gradually building up the zero coupon curve from shorter dated securities to longer dated securities.

Gilt-edged securities are traditionally bullet instruments paying six-monthly interest. Consequently, if we take a gilt which has just passed its penultimate interest date (six months to maturity), it will, in effect, be a zero coupon bond. Accordingly, its yield will be the yield on a zero coupon bond. If we then take another gilt which has also just passed its prepenultimate interest date (12 months to maturity) it will have just one interim interest payment and then the final payment of interest and principal. We can use the zero-coupon yield we calculated on the first gilt to calculate the present value of the interim interest payment on the second gilt, and this enables us to infer the zero-coupon yield the market is applying to the final maturity in 12 months' time. Repeating this basic process enables the full zero-coupon yield curve to be constructed to whatever maturity we require.

The following example to November 2001 demonstrates the approach using gilt prices prevailing on 29 March 1996. Table A.1 feratured at the end of this appendix shows the prices of various gilts, with increasing maturity down the table. The columns are fairly self-explanatory; *Redemp date* is the issue redemption date when holders are repaid £100 capital plus accumulated semi-annual interest. *Duration maturity* is modified Macaulay duration which is explained further below. *Redemp yield* is the annualized yield to redemption based on the current price and the periodic interest payments. *Next interest date* is self-explanatory and *£ due* is the amount of interest due to the holder after payment of rebate to the current seller. The zero-coupon yield curve analysis appears on the right of the table. The numbers appearing below the zero-coupon yields are the present values of the interim interest payments at the associated zero-coupon yield. All yields and zero-coupon rates are continuously discounted.

The first gilt, the 13 1/4% Exchequer Loan 1996 matures on 15 May 1996. As interest on gilts is paid semi-annually, there are no interim interest payments, and this gilt will pay capital plus accumulated semi-annual interest as a bullet repayment on maturity. If we calculate the yield on this gilt, we find a zero-coupon yield of 5.64%.

156   *Forfaiting for exporters*

The second gilt, 10% Conversion Stock 1996 matures on 15 November 1996 and makes an interim payment of interest on 15 May 1996. From the evaluation of the 13¼% Exchequer Loan we know the zero-coupon yield for May 1996 (5.64%) and we can calculate the present value of the interim interest payment on the 10% Conversion Stock (£1.28). Deducting this from the current price of the 10% Conversion Stock gives us the present value of the principal plus interest payable on maturity – equivalent to a zero-coupon payment – and this enables us to calculate the 5.84% zero-coupon yield for 15 November 1996.

We were rather lucky to find two gilts where the maturity of the first has the same date as the interim interest payments of the second. For the third gilt, the 10½% Exchequer Stock 1997, we have no such luck, and it is necessary to interpolate between the zero-coupon yields for 15 May and 15 November to find the zero-coupon yield applicable to the 21 August 1996 interim interest payment. Having found this yield to be 5.75%, we can use the same procedure as we used for the 10% Conversion Stock 1996 to calculate the 6.04% zero-coupon yield for 21 February 1997. The procedure is then simply repeated for the rest of the gilts in the list.

Figure A.3 shows the zero-coupon yield curve and the normal yield curve on a coupon-paying bond and as indicated in Figure A.2, the normal yield curve falls below the zero-coupon yield curve.

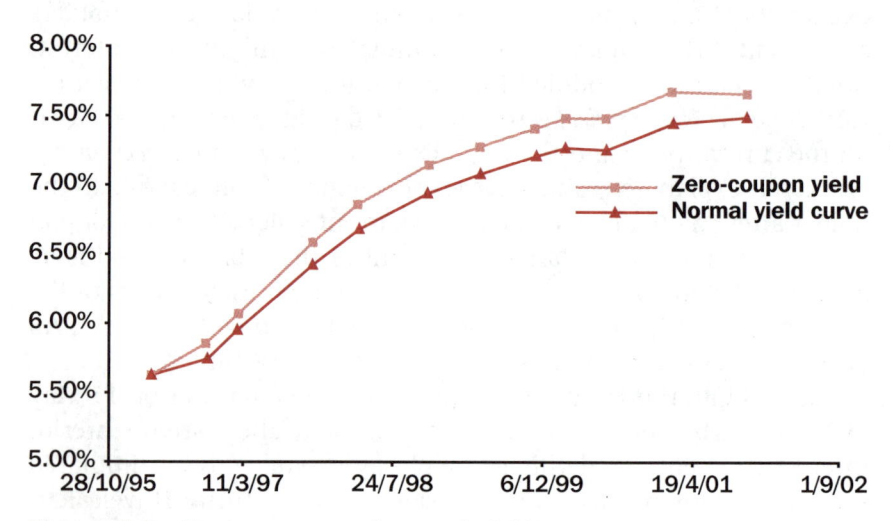

Figure A.3 Zero-coupon and normal yield curve.

The difference between the two curves is a maximum of 0.23% per annum in February 2001. Hence, using the normal yield curve instead of a zero-coupon yield curve to discount a zero-dividend bond payable at this date would cause a mispricing error of about 1 1/8% of the discounted value – a substantial real present value loss to the buyer of the paper.

As this example demonstrates, calculation of zero-coupon yield curves implies a rather tortuous procedure although the real error implied in using normal yield curves on coupon paying bonds does justify the effort. Fortunately, another procedure using modified duration considerably simplifies the calculations whilst retaining a very satisfactory degree of accuracy.

Zero-coupon yield curves analysis adjusts the periodic yield on the basis that the yield curve is not linear. Macaulay duration (1938) takes the yield on the coupon-paying gilt but adjusts the maturity to recognise the early repayment effects of interim payments of interest. It measures how long, on average, the holder of the bond has to wait before receiving the average present value dollar. The contribution of each maturity to the duration depends upon its term and contribution to the total present value. Formally duration (D) is given by

$$D = \frac{\sum_{t=1}^{n} \frac{(C_t)t}{(1+i_t)^t} + \frac{A_n}{(1+i_n)^n}}{\sum_{t=1}^{n} \frac{C_t}{(1+i_t)^t} + \frac{A}{(1+i_n)^n}} \quad (6)$$

where D is the duration, C is the value of coupon payment, A is the redemption value, t is the period of coupon payment, i is the periodic interest rate and n is the maturity period.

The denominator in equation (6) is the present value of the series of payments – the price of the security, whilst the term within the summation of the numerator is the term of each interim payment weighted by its present value.

Hopewell and Kaufman in 1973 extended the duration concept and related the interest rate sensitivity of a bond to its modified duration (D_M) defined as

158   *Forfaiting for exporters*

$$D_M = D/[1 + i/m] \qquad (7)$$

where *m* is the compounding frequency and

$$dP/P = -D_M dr \qquad (8)$$

where *dP/P* is the percentage price change.

Bonds with equal modified durations have equal sensitivities to changes in interest rates. Modified duration has the effect of encapsulating the interest rate sensitivities of a bond and equating them to the interest rate sensitivity of a zero-coupon bond. Hence plotting a yield curve as a function of modified duration enables us to identify the yield applicable to a zero-coupon bond of equivalent maturity. This calculation is performed in Table A.1. Note that the duration maturity of the exchequer loan 1996 maturity 15/5/96 is equal to its redemption date, this is because there are no interim payments of principal. In theory, each interim payment should be discounted at the applicable zero coupon rate; however, in practice, duration is not particularly sensitive to the variation of rates across the yield curve and the total yield on the security can safely be used as a proxy. Table A.2 at the end of this appendix calculates the zero-coupon yields, duration based yields and normal yields for equivalent maturities and these are shown in Figure A.4.

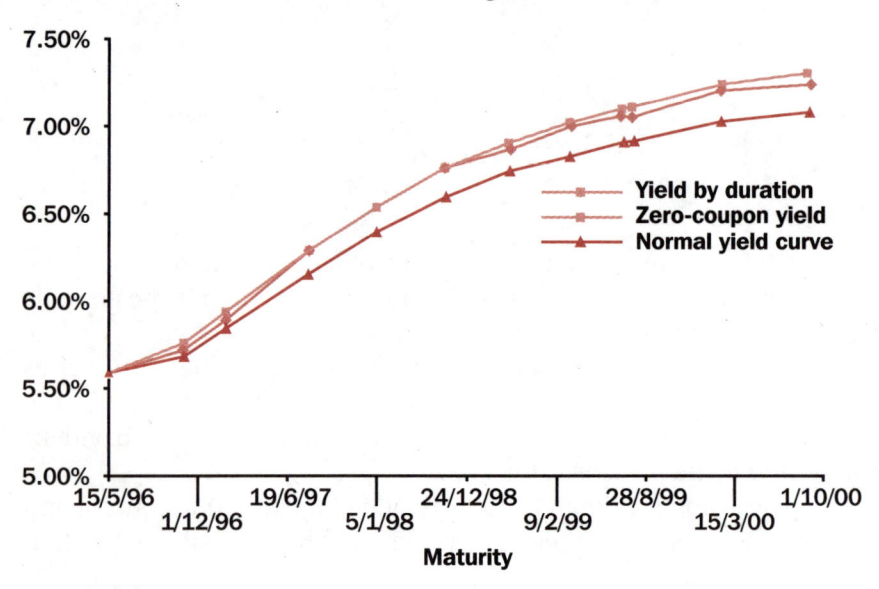

Figure A.4 Zero-coupon/duration-based yield curves.

Adjusting the maturity to the modified duration has the effect of shifting the normal yield curve to the left, such that it closely follows the zero-coupon yield curve. The principal advantage of this procedure is its simplicity and relative accuracy. Popular spreadsheet packages are supplied with standard functions for calculating bond yields and modified duration.

Table A.2 calculates the error in using the duration and normal yield curve relative to using the correct zero-coupon yield curve. The *Error* column is the difference between the zero-coupon calculation and the duration or normal yield curve method. *Estimat err* % expresses this as a percentage of the difference between the short- and long-term yield, i.e. the increase in rates across the yield curve. This is a measure of the accuracy of the method to capture the variation of interest rates. Whereas the normal yield curve has a maximum but increasing error of 15% of the variation of interest rates, the modified duration method gives a result within 5% of the correct value.

Conclusion

In this appendix we have highlighted the importance of using appropriately derived yield curves for discounting zero-coupon paper. The zero-coupon yield curve is the most accurate approach but good approximations can easily be obtained using modified duration. Both of these approaches are superior to using standard coupon-paying yield curves.

Having ascertained the appropriate discount rate, continuous discounting provides a flexible and simple method of calculating discounted values. In combination these analytical techniques provide essential tools for discounting trade paper.

Table A.1 Zero-coupon yield curve analysis

Redemp date	Coupon	Stock	Price 29.3.96	£MM	Duration maturity	Redemp yield	Next interest date	£ due
15/05/96	13¼%	Excheqeur Loan 1996	101	800	15/05/96	5.64%	15/05/96	1.71
15/11/96	10%	Conversion Stock 1996	102¹⁵/₃₂	3,409	29/10.96	5.75%	15/05/96	1.29
21/02/97	10½%	Exchequer Stock 1997	103¾	3,700	01/02/97	5.95%	21/08/96	4.17
27 Oct 97	15%	Exchequer Stock 1997	112⅜	830	03/08/97	6.40%	27/04/96	1.19
30/03/98	7¼%	Treasury Stock 1998	100¹¹/₁₆	8,150	05.01/98	6.65%	30/09/96	3.67
20/11/98	12%	Exchequer Stock 1998	111¹⁵/₃₂	3,909	08/06/98	6.91%	20/05/96	1.71
19/05/99	10½%	Treasury Stock 1999	108⅞	1,252	29/10/98	7.03%	19/05/96	1.47
22/11/99	10¼%	Conversion Stock 1999	108⅞	1,798	11/03/99	7.16%	22/05/96	1.52
03/03/00	9%	Converstion Stock 2000	105¹/₁₆	5,358	05/07/99	7.22%	03/09/96	3.90
14/07/00	13%	Treasury Stock 2000	119¹⁵/₁₆	3,171	20/07/99	7.21%	24/07/96	3.81
26/02/01	10%	Treasury Stock 2001	109⅜	4,406	08/02/00	7.39%	26/08/96	4.11
06/11/01	7%	Treasury Stock 2001	96²⁵/₃₂	10,750	26/08/00	7.43%	06/11/96	4.26

*Interest due is adjusted for amount of rebate to seller, which depends on days since last coupon payment. Valuation date 29 March 1996.

Appendix 161

Zero coupon bond yields/coupon present values, by coupon date

6	15/11/96

	5.84%								
6	21/02/97								
	6.04%								

	27/10/96	27/04/97	27/10/97						
6	5.82%	6.17%	6.55%						

	7.25	7.02							
6	30/03/97	30/09/97	30/03/98						
	5.99%	6.49%	6.81%						

	3.41	3.29							
6	20/11/96	20/05/97	20/11/97	20/05/98	20/11/98				
	5.84%	6.22%	6.60%	6.89%	7.10%				

	5.78	5.59	5.38	5.18					
6	19/11/96	19/05/97	19/11/97	19/05/98	19/11/98	19/05/99			
	5.84%	6.22%	6.60%	5.89%	7.10%	7.23%			

	5.06	4.89	4.71	4.53	4.35				
6	22/11/96	22/05/97	22/11/97	22/05/98	22/11/98	22/05/99	22/11/99		
	5.85%	6.22%	6.61%	6.89%	7.10%	7.23%	7.37%		

	4.93	4.77	4.60	4.42	4.25	4.08			
6	03/03/97	03/09/97	03/03/98	03/09/98	03/03/99	03/09/99	03/03/00		
	5.96%	6.44%	6.82%	7.07%	7.22%	7.31%	7.43%		

	4.26	4.10	3.95	3.79	3.64	3.50			
6	14/01/97	14/07/97	14/01/98	14/07/98	14/01/99	14/07/99	14/01/00	14/07/00	
	5.91%	6.33%	6.72%	6.98%	7.16%	7.27%	7.40%	7.44%	

	6.20	5.99	5.76	5.54	5.32	5.12	4.91		
6	26/02/97	26/08/97	26/02/98	26/08/98	26/02/99	26/08/99	26/02/00	26/08/00	26/02/01
	5.95%	6.42%	6.81%	7.05%	7.22%	7.30%	7.44%	7.45%	7.62%

	4.73	4.57	4.39	4.22	4.05	3.90	3.74	3.60		
6	06/05/97	06/11/97	06/05/98	06/11/98	06/05/99	06/11/99	06/05/00	06/11/00	06/05/01	06/11/01
	6.03%	6.57%	6.95%	7.17%	7.30%	7.35%	7.49%	7.45%	9.09%	7.59%

	3.27	3.15	3.02	2.90	2.79	2.68	2.57	2.48	2.20	

Table A.2 Zero coupon, duration yields and coupon-paying bonds yields over standard maturities

Maturity	Stock	Duration method					Standard yield			
		Coupon-paying zero coupon								
		Duration	Bond yield	For duration	Error	Estimat err %	Duration	For duration	Error	Estimat err %
15 May 96	Exchequer Loan 1996	15/05/96	5.64%	5.64%	0%	−0.01%	15/05/96	5.64%	0%	0.00%
15 Nov 96	Conversion Stock 1996	29/10/96	5.75%	5.82%	−1/16%	−4.52%	29/10/96	5.74%	−1/16%	−5.19%
21 Feb 97	Exchequer Stock 1997	01/02/97	5.95%	6.00%	−1/32%	−3.27%	01/02/97	5.91%	−1/16%	−5.85%
27 Oct 97	Exchequer Stock 1997	03/08/97	6.40%	6.38%	0%	1.33%	03/08/97	6.25%	−1/8%	−8.68%
30 Mar 98	Treasury Stock 1998	05/01/98	6.65%	6.67%	0%	−1.24%	05/01/98	6.51%	−1.8%	−10.21%
20 Nov 98	Exchequer Stock 1998	08/06/98	6.91%	6.89%	0%	0.84%	08/06/98	6.73%	−5/32%	−10.96%
19 May 99	Treasury Stock 1999	29/10/98	7.03%	7.07%	−1/32%	−2.84%	29/10/98	6.88%	−5.32%	−12.26%
22 Nov 99	Conversion Stock 1999	11/03/99	7.16%	7.18%	0%	−1.20%	11/03/99	6.98%	−3/16%	−12.91%
03 Mar 00	Conversion Stock 2000	05/07/99	7.22%	7.26%	−1/32%	−2.92%	05/07/99	7.06%	3/16%	13.31%
14 Jul 00	Treasury Stock 2000	20/07/99	7.21%	7.27%	−1/16%	−4.16%	20/07/99	7.07%	−3/16%	−13.35%
26 Feb 01	Treasury Stock 2001	08/02/00	7.39%	7.42%	0%	−1.75%	08/02/00	7.21%	−3/16%	−13.91%
06 Nov 01	Treasury Stock 2001	26/08/00	7.43%	7.49%	−1/32%	−4.06%	26/08/00	7.26%	−7/32%	−15.59%

Index

Accounting
 rules 95–97
 time periods 98
 strategies 105
Accounting Standards Boards'
 Statements of Standard
 Accounting Practice (SSAP)
 141
Asset value 16, 17, 44, 102–105
Aval 67, 74, 75, 78
Avalizing bank 62, 74, 116, 147
Avalizor 145

Bagley, Andrew 151
Bank guarantee 12, 22, 31–32, 59, 116
Bank of England 87
Bank receivables 1, 4, 72
Bid 115
Bills of Exchange Act 1882: 138
bills of exchange 3, 4, 8, 30–31, 65, 67–70, 145
 present value, of note 8
bills of lading 75, 145
book receivables 65
book-keeping 93–95
burgschaft 66, 74–75, 80, 145

Capital
 goods 2, 6, 13, 142
 payout method 50
 value 47, 50
Cash flow, discounting 18–19, 20, 35
Certificate of inspection 146
Certificate of origin 146

Closing stock valuation 98–99
Comecon trading bloc 7
Commercial invoice 146
Commitment 109, 112, 114, 115, 146
 fee 146
 period 34, 146
Communist bloc 6
Communist economies 6
Compound interest 17–18, 20, 44, 151–153
Confirmation 78–80
 cost 79
 full 78–80
 silent 78–80
Contingent liabilities 80–81, 146
Contracts 109, 114
 commodity 2
 short-term
 spare parts 2
Cost of funds yield curve 42–43
Counter-party 146
 risk 85
Credit
 buyer 67
 instruments 3, 4
  non-recourse 1
 margin 43, 48, 50, 52, 55, 59, 146
 period 34
 risk 4, 8, 55–60
 supplier 66
Credit-conforming documentation 76, 77, 79, 80
Current market price *see* Present value

Days of grace 30, 146
Deferred payment
  letters of credit 3, 4, 66, 77
Delivery period 34
Discount house 5
Discount rate 5, 8, 20, 29–30, 146, 153
  risk 41–60
  straight 37
Discount to yield rate 28, 36, 143
Discounting
  cash flows 18–19, 20, 35
  methods 28, 35–38, 41
Documentary collection 147
Documentation 5, 8, 61–86, 116–118, 139–140
  covering 74–80
  risk 61–64
  transport 64–65

East Europe 2, 9
East–West European trade 2, 9, 14, 80, 131
Economic value 15–16
Emerging markets 2, 33
Eurobond market 33
Exchange rate
  risk 5
Export Credit Guarantee Department (ECGD) 110, 135, 147
Export credit agencies (ECA) 147
Exporter 9, 10, 12, 32, 38–39, 55–56, 109–118
Exporter rate 60

Face value 23, 41, 147
Fee period 34, 148
Financial instruments *see also* Negotiable instruments, 6, 19, 33, 65–7, 134–7
  versus trade 137, 139
Financial Reporting Standards 16

Financial Reporting Statements (FRS) 141
Fixed rate notes 143
  conversion to floating rate 48–53
Fixed-rate loans 51–2
Floating rate promissory notes 46–7
  conversion from fixed rate 48–53
Forfaiting
  benefits of 12
  defining characteristics of 6
  definition of 1
  documentation 61–80
  growth of 11–12
  guide 109–18
  history of 2–14
  houses 11
  market
    primary 11–12, 31–2, 34,140
    secondary 10–11, 31–2, 33, 34,140
    size 87–91
  other terms for 3
  proposal 23–5
Free title
  assignment of 11

Geneva Convention 7, 69, 74, 138
Guarantee fee 5, 147
Guarantees 5, 20, 66, 73
Guarantor 23, 24, 26, 74

House of Lords 141

Import licence 147
Importers 9, 10, 12, 55–6, 57
Inland trade bill 4–5
Interest rate 5, 17–18, 20
  movement 5
  risk 5, 8, 41–60, 148
Internal rate of return 19

International Chamber of
    Commerce Uniform Customs
    and Practice 86
International Convention of
    Commercial Bills 7, 69, 138
IOU 2, 4

Legal issues 137–8
Letters of credit (L/Cs) 75–80
    acceptance 77
    conformation 78–80
    deferred payment 3, 66, 77
    sight 66, 76
    stand by 78
London Forfaiting Company PLC
    11, 90
London Interbank Offered Rate
    (LIBOR) 29, 42, 148

Manufacturing period 34
Market value 15, 16, 102–5
Maturity date 2, 19, 30, 148

Negotiable instruments 1, 24, 80,
    148
    non-recourse 16, 31, 81
    secondary market 10–11
    trade credit 6
Net present value 18–19, 35
Non-recourse trade finance 1, 2, 3,
    11, 12, 13, 25, 27, 31, 33, 43,
    55, 56, 61, 64, 67, 81, 87–91,
    102, 131–43
    definition 1, 131
    growth 11–12, 131–43
    history 2–13
    promissory note 15, 16, 18, 30,
        80, 124

Obligator 1, 7
Option 109, 113, 148
Organization for Economic and
    Commercial Development
    (OECD) 12

Pacioli 93
Papoutes, Stathis 11
Payment 2, 3–4, 5, 6, 30, 56, 66, 89,
    110, 112, 117, 119, 121, 122,
    129, 133–5, 151–8
Phoenician traders 2–3, 6
Present value 19–20, 35–7, 38, 41
Promissory notes 3, 4, 8, 30, 41, 43,
    46–7, 51, 52, 65, 71–2, 119,
    126, 143, 148
    floating rate 46–4

rate of return
    internal 19
risk
    credit 5, 55–60
    bank guarantee 59
    documentation 5, 61–86
    exchange rate 5
    interest rate 5, 41–53
    country 57–59
    transaction 81
    payout 82–83

Safe custody 84
Semi-annual discount to yield 23,
    41, 125, 149
Shipment 116–118
    date 149
Short-term funding 13
Silent confirmation 78–80, 149

Taxation 141
Tenor 5, 43, 45, 47, 50, 60, 149
Terms and conditions 25–8
    calculation 23–5
    example of 21–2
    flexibility of 43
    future of 131–43
Time value 17–18
Trade
    credit 1, 3, 6–7
    debt 139
Trade instrument 3, 10, 133

Trading period 94, 98
Transferable note 6, 32

Uniform Customs and Practices
    Document Credits (UCP500)
    77

Value date 149–50

West European manufacturers 2, 6,
    14, 80, 131

West, Mark 50
Western technology 2, 6
Wilson, Jack 11
Without-recourse
    debt 150
    financing 3, 133, 143

Zero coupon yield curves 154–9,
    160–1, 162